ENERGY
INDEPENDENCE

ENERGY INDEPENDENCE

YOUR EVERYDAY GUIDE TO REDUCING FUEL CONSUMPTION

Christine Woodside

The Lyons Press
Guilford, Connecticut

An imprint of The Globe Pequot Press

To buy books in quantity for corporate use
or incentives, call **(800) 962–0973**
or e-mail **premiums@GlobePequot.com.**

The Lyons Press is an imprint of The Globe Pequot Press.

Designed by Sheryl P. Kober

The Library of Congress has previously cataloged an earlier edition as follows:

Woodside, Christine, 1959–
The homeowner's guide to energy independence : alternative power sources for the average American / Christine Woodside.
    p. cm.
ISBN 978-1-59921-528-0
Dwellings—Energy conservation. 2. Electric power production. 3. Dwellings—Electric equipment. 4. Ecological houses. I. Title.
TJ163.5.D86W674 2005
333.79—dc22

                2005028063

Printed in the United States of America

10 9 8 7 6 5 4 3 2 1

THANKS TO . . .

Holly Rubino, who edited this edition

Lilly Golden, who edited the first edition

Rene Ebersole of *Audubon* magazine

Bud Ward of yaleclimatemediaforum.org

Jim Motavalli of *E* magazine

Jim Schembari and Ned Kilkelly of the *New York Times*

Tom Condon of the *Hartford Courant*

Russell Powell of *New England Watershed* magazine

The editors of *Yale Alumni* magazine

Elizabeth Eddy for the hybrid car chart

Nat Eddy for the solar photovoltaic explanation

Darlene Mariani for research

Annie Eddy for advice and research

My mother, Gloria Woodside, for strong-arming bookstores to carry the book

Valerie Fales, Priscilla Martel, and Lynn Cochrane

Martha Lyon

Bill Chatman

CONTENTS

Reading the headlines can leave ordinary people feeling helpless about the amount of fossil fuel we burn and our dependence on foreign countries (some of them not so friendly) for it.
Have you ever felt like declaring your independence?

Petroleum rules, and coal is tied with natural gas for second
place. All three have accelerated world climate change. Starting
roughly forty years from now, something must take their place.

From President Carter's solar panels on the White House roof to
NASA's newest solar panels, the technology for harnessing the
sun has dramatically improved. A look at how they work, how to
start small, the estimated costs (both financial and environmental), and the amount of time it takes to recoup your investment.

What are wind generators and how do they work? A primer
on wind power on a large scale. How to start small, how to
deal with the neighbors, products, and costs, and the amount
of time it takes to recoup your investment.

While the predictions of a hydrogen economy still resemble a
science fiction story, fuel cells have made some progress. How
do they work, and where can you buy one? Biodiesel fuel for
cars or furnaces (primarily vegetable oil) has become an industry. Geothermal systems tap into a constant natural temperature below the ground.

INTRODUCTION

Why You Need This Book

In the three years since the first edition of this book appeared, a kind of citizen energy consciousness has rooted itself in America. We now know too much to make fun of alternative energy as something for latter-day hippies living in yurts. This latest energy awakening really started in the late 1990s, when electricity supplies faltered during high-use summer periods. Then in late 2004 the price of crude oil started to rise, and since 2007 it has shot into ranges previously unimaginable. The shock of $40-per-barrel oil in 2004 became $60, $100, and, by July 2008, above $140 before it began to slide again.

Travelers began the 2005 summer season with $2.10-per-gallon gasoline, which seemed low a few months later, when Hurricane Katrina pushed prices to more than $3.00. This, in turn, seemed a bargain when economic instability and the unresolved war in Iraq pushed the price to more than $4.00 per gallon.

Clearly we live in volatile times energy-wise. Although oil is still cheaper than harnessing most alternative forms of energy, like the sun and wind, the reality of cheap oil has started to lose its footing. This is not simply due to supplies and cost. The major cause of accelerated climate change, something we have observed for many decades, has become indisputable among scientists: fossil-fuel burning by humans.[1] This leaves ordinary people and policymakers to ask how the consumer-driven way of life can scale itself back.

Many factors, from economic predictions to political tensions to war, influence oil prices. But one factor is coming into ever-sharper focus: The world's oil reserves are dipping ever lower, and sometime in the next couple of generations, they won't be the cheapest and most efficient way to power the majority of society.

We have dealt with short-term problems, such as a few unusually cold winters when people burned more petroleum than usual just when oil producers tried to cut their costs. More ominous are the long-term trends. Petroleum, natural gas, and coal are all finite resources. Demand for them is ever rising, particularly as the world population continues to grow, China continues its roller-coaster ride into the first world, and the United States continues to use a quarter of the world's energy. Political leaders have known about all of these problems for years. And yet, despite the great interest in renewable energy and conservation by ever-increasing numbers of ordinary citizens like you and me, the country seems stuck in a state of anxiety. We have yet to take major action.[2]

Gas for our cars now costs more than the inflation-adjusted price of the late 1970s. Even when adjusted for inflation, crude oil in 2008 reached historic highs of $140 per barrel before dropping again to under $100. This volatility stands up to what we experienced in 1979 (when it cost $38 per barrel or roughly $107 in today's money) or in 1864 ($8 per barrel or about $134 in today's money).[3]

How desperate do we want to be before we look for other ways to power our lives, keep warm, and travel? Ordinary people are starting to ask why we must rely on a supply of oil that will run out in their children's lifetimes to provide basic needs like heat and hot water. Experts predict that in the next half-century, petroleum reserves will reach a point too low to yield a benefit. As we approach that point, petroleum will continue to cost ever more as demand rises and extraction becomes more challenging.

The United States relies on several other countries to supply our oil: Canada, Saudi Arabia, Mexico, Nigeria, Venezuela, and a few others that include Kuwait and Iraq, with which we have gone to war. Listening to the evening news can leave the average American feeling helpless about our dependence on foreign countries in unstable areas for that most basic need—fuel.

So far I have been talking economics—the supply, demand, and costs of the relatively near future—and making the argument that this instability should convince most of us to change how we plan to use energy in the coming years. There is a much greater reason, of course, for us to change our ways—one that I sometimes hesitate to invoke because it can be tempting to believe only what suits us if we doubt the guesswork of even the smartest scientists. That is, of course, the toll the pace of modern energy use has exacted on the planet. First of all, we are using up ancient stores of energy too fast to show much consideration for the coming centuries. More important, the burning of fossil fuels is linked with the quickening trend of global warming. The Earth has gone through warming and cooling periods in its very, very long history, most of which doesn't involve us. But in the last century, a warming trend has accelerated dramatically. It is now an indisputable fact that this accelerated rise in the average yearly temperature on Earth over the past century is the result of humans releasing large amounts of carbon dioxide and other greenhouse gases into the atmosphere by burning oil, coal, and natural gas. Most of North America's electricity generation, home heating, and transportation rely on fossil fuels. Until we use and develop alternatives, we will continue to feed our precious resources into the hopper of unnatural, human-caused, accelerated warming.

Have you ever felt like pulling away from this dependence on fossil fuels? I have, and yet when I started considering this a few years ago, I realized I didn't know the first thing about how to do it. I was, and largely remain, an average East Coast dweller burning up fossil fuel in my car and in my house and applauding, from afar, off-grid handymen and people rich enough to buy two banks of solar panels. I'm changing, but I have learned that such change comes incrementally.

My husband, our two daughters, and I are neither handymen nor wealthy. We live in a 1,100-square-foot Victorian house in a tiny Connecticut town. My family considers itself frugal and environmentally conscious. We keep the thermostat low, turn it down at night, and turn off the lights when we go to sleep. We aren't big television watchers. We have one home computer and no microwave. We cook from scratch on a propane stove and use a water-saving shower nozzle. Needless to say, I felt irritated and powerless when utility deregulation and supply shortages started to affect my region of the country a few years ago, and I started to pay closer attention to our electric bills.

One of our bills for one month, between mid-January and mid-February 2005, came to $216.37 for 1,694 kilowatt-hours of power. (Including all of the transmission and distribution surcharges in my state, the rate at that time was almost 13 cents per kilowatt-hour. Since then it has risen to almost 19 cents per kilowatt-hour.) In southern New England, nuclear and oil-burning plants still provide much of the electricity. But this story of rising power demand and uncertain energy supplies is playing out in varying ways across the country. My family's skyrocketing bills—roughly twice what we had paid only five years earlier—forced me to consider our electricity and where it comes from. I quickly learned that we were paying not only much more than we had budgeted, but that we were using almost twice as much electricity as the average household in our state, even though we have a small house and don't heat with electricity. (We heat with an oil-burning furnace.) It was a puzzle to us, but it appeared that our electric hot-water heater was the main culprit.

The same month, I talked to Ed Witkin, who at the time lived west of me in Bridgewater, Connecticut, with his wife, Ellen Shrader, and their two daughters. Their modern house ran almost entirely on solar energy. They were not connected to the electric grid; no wires extended up their long driveway from the street to their house. Forced by their own choice to be careful with power, they had settled into a routine of using no more than 150 kilowatt-hours a month. The Witkin-Shrader family was the same size as ours—two adults and two teenage daughters—and the house itself was larger than ours. They were using one-tenth of what we were in the winter (which is our highest use time because we don't have air-conditioning). They weren't sitting in the dark, washing in frigid water, or cooking on an open fire. Like my family they owned one computer and did without a microwave. Their daughters took long, hot showers just as ours did, they had a propane kitchen stove similar to ours, and they, too, watched little television.

Here is where they differed from us: Their refrigerator (a Sun Frost) was an ultra-low-energy brand, while ours was not; they heated water with solar collectors on their roof, while we heated our water with electricity; they used compact fluorescent bulbs in all of their fixtures, while we had only two in our house. My family was using more than ten times the energy they were. This realization that I wasn't the au naturel, environmentally conscious woman I'd envisioned made me feel like a guest on *Candid Camera*, in which I'd first told some stranger on the street that I probably used less electricity than everyone I knew, only to find that I was a bad statistic.

What was up? We, like most Americans, were hooked on a way of life that used too much energy. We might not be wasteful people by nature, but we were going about our business without the feeling that we should turn things off. We didn't consider it an emergency to replace our ten-year-old refrigerator. We thought that someday we'd get around to replacing the bulbs. We sometimes forgot to turn off lights and appliances. The Witkin-Shraders paid attention to everything, because they were collecting their own energy at their house and didn't want to run out. We, on the other hand, knew that more energy would always be there for us, as long as we were willing to pay for it.

My husband and I had to face up to the fact that we were not doing enough by living in a small house and holding onto old appliances like our vintage 1993 refrigerator, which used four times the energy of many available new models. Our top-loading washing machine was even older, but because it still operated, we didn't want to discard it even though it used far more power and water than the new front-loading tumble washers. We relied on what we thought was an efficient electric water heater, bought only a few years ago. But then we started to believe that heating water with electricity is wasteful.

Until that year when I compared my house to the Witkin-Shraders', I did not realize that a family like mine could reduce our dependence on fossil fuels. I have since realized that our 1,100-square-foot Victorian house could drastically cut its energy consumption. At a grassroots level all of us can begin to change the world by refusing to depend solely on distant sources of fossil fuels. It makes sense morally, financially, and, most of all, environmentally.

How do we do it? Making the move to using less energy isn't an easy choice in financial terms, for us and for most middle-class people. But I'm pleased to say that my family has made major changes in just a few years, and yours can too. One year we bought a new refrigerator, the lowest-energy Maytag I could find. The next year we replaced the washer with a tumble-style Frigidaire. Both were a little more expensive than what we were used to, but we immediately saw the savings in our electric bills. We replaced most of the lightbulbs in the house with compact-fluorescent bulbs. We are reducing our fossil-fuel usage step-by-step. We didn't want to just sit back and wait for the large utilities to start using solar or wind power and thus make changes for us. (In fact our state, like many states, has added surcharges that enable it to put money into renewable sources, which means that officials are starting to help us move toward renewables, no matter how slowly that transition might be.) We took action ourselves.

So what happened to our energy use? We've done okay in three years. The electric bill covering the period from mid-January to mid-February 2008 was $191.65 for 1,071 kilowatt-hours. That month we owed roughly 11.5 percent less than for the same month in 2005, even though the rate (including the delivery surcharges) had increased by more than 38 percent. More important was our reduction in energy use by almost 37 percent. We have yet to replace our hot-water heater, so I know that we can improve on our record so far.

So far most of our changes have been to conserve energy. But what about installing equipment to gather energy from the sun, wind, a stream, or underground? These technologies are now available to home and apartment dwellers. How quickly can consumers recoup investments in alternative energy sources? My family is starting to consider these technologies as they enter the realm of affordability. Because electricity is now about 19 cents per kilowatt-hour in Connecticut, it appears a photovoltaic system would pay for itself in only four to eight years. Efficient appliances can pay for themselves in a few years. Gas-electric hybrid cars can pay for themselves in even less time, depending on the model you choose. Yes, we would get that money back, and yes, we would begin to get away from the old ways as soon as we made these choices. In almost all cases, you would eventually recoup your investment. Environmentally, you and the rest of the planet begin to receive benefits the second you make the switch.

Don't wait for alternative energy to become mainstream. Take steps as an individual now and create the demand for alternative energy that assures it will become mainstream. Whether you live alone or with others, in the city, the suburbs, or the country, you can take steps toward independence immediately. We use more power than necessary. We must stop looking at alternative energy as deficient because it could never provide enough energy to directly substitute for oil. Yes, we can use alternative energy sources instead of oil, but we also have to commit to using less energy overall.

You can save money in the long term by spending money in the short term. Begin by using less energy as my family and I did—by changing your behavior and changing, little by little, your appliances and sources of heat and light (see chapters 9 and 10). Next, experiment with the two most viable and affordable alternative energy sources: solar panels or solar-thermal systems, and wind generators, which I discuss in chapters 2 and 3. Consider these fuels, developing technologies, and strategies, which I cover in chapters 4 through 9: geothermal heat pumps, biodiesel fuel, fuel cells, wood, micro-hydroelectric systems, alternative cars, and alternatives to driving.

The most important thing you can do, however, is this: Use less energy—an act you can accomplish quickly and that's necessary when using most alternative energy sources. While conservation has yet to catch on as a habit in the United States, we must learn to conserve energy in a time when energy companies are venturing into deeper and more complicated places to find oil, natural gas, and coal, and when worry in the marketplace has made prices of basic energy so high that it will disrupt our daily lives from here on out. It's the most basic and important act we can perform. I have realized that the best way to conserve energy is to force ourselves into crisis mode. This means believing, as our parents did during hard times, that every car trip, every twirl of the thermostat, every push of the light switch, every decision to buy an appliance, every choice about home-improvement projects, connects not to some do-gooder mentality per se, but to crucial necessity to reduce energy use. We must learn to think of conservation as our response to a crisis that the country has been slow to accept and even slower to act on.

It's not hard to conserve, but it means we have to go against the grain of our friends and family and start thinking differently. High on my list, now that we have a lower-energy refrigerator and washer and use compact fluorescents, is to limit my use of hot water by taking shorter showers and not leaving the water running while I rinse dishes, to explore trimming the tops of a few critical trees to install a solar hot-water system on our roof, to replace my old Ford Taurus with a used Volkswagen Golf (combining low cost with fairly high gas mileage) or, perhaps, even a hybrid, and to drive fewer miles.

As Thomas L. Friedman, columnist for the *New York Times,* said in a speech at Brown University in 2008, it doesn't really matter whether we reduce energy use because of climate change or because of dwindling world supplies. What matters is that we reduce energy use. Just a few years ago, those most likely to aggressively conserve energy were those who viewed it as a matter of environmental ethics. Now the ethics of saving energy is beginning to converge with the economics of doing so. In a sense I couldn't be happier that my friends and acquaintances are talking about climate change and energy prices, because I can see that everyone is starting to care. It might sound a little cynical to look at things as Friedman does, but I daresay he's right: What matters is that we reduce energy use, period.

We, the people, can force the issue, and we can do this now.

CHAPTER ONE

The Situation Today: Oil Still Rules

America depends on fossil fuels, particularly oil, to support life as we know it. Fossil fuels provide about 85 percent of the world's energy sources. Petroleum is the largest pool, providing about 40 percent. Nearly tied for second place are natural gas (about 23 percent) and coal (about 22 percent). It remains relatively cheap to find and use fossil fuels.[1] These fossil fuels provide the vast majority of energy for electricity, heat, and transportation in houses, apartments, and industry. But they can't do this indefinitely. Experts have predicted that petroleum reserves will peter out in around 2050.[2]

Such predictions have been widely touted for decades, but as a nation, Americans have only recently begun to worry, and, so far, our worry hasn't translated into a reduction of our demand for fossil fuel. We have not made the connection between our own habits, actions, and needs and the diminishing fuel reserves that fulfill them. We have lived with incredible plentitude for half a century.

The federal government is wrestling with a long-term energy policy. It has been inconsistent in diverting tax money to subsidize alternative energy; some years it has, and some years it hasn't. More traditional fuels have enjoyed steady policies of subsidies. The wind-power industry, for example, has suffered with the wavering policies about government subsidies, and the solar-photovoltaic industry has benefited largely from state rebates and other incentives. Nevertheless, leaders tell citizens to conserve energy, because they can't ignore the disconnect between Americans' consumption and our reliance on foreign oil. In 2007, the first time since the mid-1970s, Congress passed legislation on car mileage, setting a standard of 35 miles per gallon by 2020 averaged over the whole fleet of cars, including light trucks that are so often marketed as "family cars." The new law also calls for an increase in ethanol production, to 36 billion gallons by 2022, or four times the amount called for in 2008, and more efficient lighting, with plans to make the incandescent lightbulb obsolete. The 2007 law did not renew subsidies for alternative energy such as wind, solar, and geothermal power that would have been covered by higher taxes on oil companies. Also absent from its final version was a proposal to require power companies to use more renewable sources. (See the sidebar, Highlights of the Energy Independence and Security Act of 2007, on page 13.)[3]

You can get upset about how slow policies have been to change, or be patient about America's predicament, but you can't deny the ordinary American's part in this situation. We rely on fossil fuels to feed not only industry and transportation but our own habits—our way of life.

Consider also the clear links scientists have established between fossil-fuel burning and the global-warming trend of the last fifty years. The fundamentally damaging aspect of fossil fuels is that when they burn, they release carbon that was stored in the ground millions of years ago. Fossil fuels form in the earth over a period of millions of years through slow decomposition and change. It does not appear that people can speed up that process to make more petroleum, coal, or natural gas. Today when scientists and policy makers argue about fossil fuels and global warming, they seem to argue most about how much we should worry about the dwindling supplies. No one argues that fossil fuels won't eventually run out. They will.

But just how soon will they run out?

Coal

Coal is fossilized peat, or very old remains of plants that were originally wet in a bog or marsh. It burns easily and is plentiful in North America. The United States holds a quarter of the world's coal reserves. Coal comes in different forms: About half of it is bituminous and anthracite coal; the other half is subbituminous and lignite coal. The air pollution caused by burning coal, especially particulate pollution, has continued to cause health and visibility problems. Technology hasn't been able to completely clean up coal, which is too bad, because the supply is plentiful. The pollution from coal-fired power plants in the Midwest and car and truck traffic has created haze over a good part of the East Coast.

Scientists predict that at the current rate of consumption, coal supplies will probably last a long time—at least another 250 years. But if the demand for coal were increased, that number could go way down. America has increased production of its plentiful coal supply and—while plans get shelved for new coal power plants here—has begun to export more coal to meet demands in China, India, and other countries that are now building coal power plants. In 2007 the United States exported 59 million tons of coal, up from 49 million the year before. The industry is predicting that exports will rise further to 120 million tons per year.[4]

The growing demand for coal is going to make it much harder for the world to limit the acceleration of climate change unless technologies to burn coal more cleanly become available quickly. One method gaining serious attention is carbon dioxide capture and storage, in which carbon dioxide emitted from burning coal is pumped underground.[5] Another method, met with some skepticism in many corners, is coal gasification, an energy-intensive and expensive process that converts coal to a gas. Germany used liquified coal during World War II, and now several countries are exploring both liquified coal and gasification. Watch the news for developments on this controversial front.

Oil

The major fuel source in the United States is oil, by which I mean petroleum.[6] Oil is old stuff. It formed over a period of millions of years, when the remains of plants and animal carcasses washed into the oceans and, with sand, piled up in layers. Pressure changed the sand to rock, while the organic material changed into petroleum. Oil combines hydrogen and carbon molecules. It travels or seeps up from the rock crevices where it formed, through tiny holes in the rock, or it remains trapped in underground oil reservoirs.[7] We are now living in a time when world demand, economics, and dwindling supplies point to the end of the oil age. It won't happen in this lifetime, but it's on the way.

Many geologists believe the basic tenets of a theory known as the peak oil theory, which holds that when half of an oil field has been pumped, the ability to extract the remaining half becomes extremely difficult. (I discuss this more later on.) Many people now argue that the world hit its peak oil production around 2005, but regardless, demand is breathing down the neck of supply, creating anxiety in the marketplace that every consumer has felt at the gas pumps and when paying oil bills.

Since petroleum overtook coal as the world's major energy source in the mid-twentieth century, the amounts people consumed have dwarfed those of coal, natural gas, nuclear power, wood, hydroelectric power, and everything else that makes energy.[8] Oil companies' geologists are working as hard as they ever have to find and extract the world's remaining petroleum in ways that don't use more resources than they collect.

It is true that a tremendous amount of oil remains trapped deep in the planet and under the oceans, but how much *recoverable* oil remains depends on whether it can be gotten at all or whether it's cost-effective to get it. Much of what remains lies trapped in rock and sand miles below the ocean floor. But, if we are able to extract it, we need to figure out if burning petroleum in the amounts the growing population *wants* makes sense for the increasing carbon dioxide in the atmosphere, which is now linked to a warming climate.

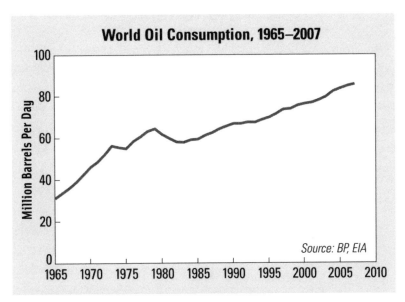

World oil consumption continues its steady increase. (Courtesy of Worldwatch Institute, *Vital Signs Online*, www.worldwatch.org)

Oil Consumption, 1950–2007

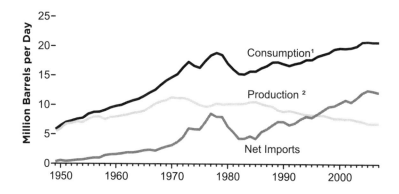

Except for during energy crises, Americans have continued to consume more petroleum products every year for the last half-century. Imports make up for the drop in domestic production. (Courtesy of U.S. Energy Information Administration)

World Oil Production, 1965–2007

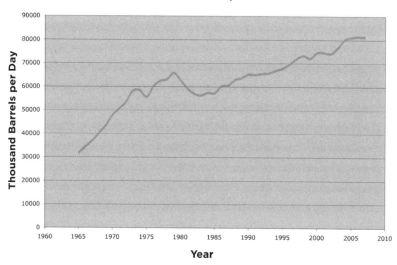

World oil production has risen steadily over the last four decades, dipping just four times, the most recent drop in 2007. (Chart by the author using data from BP)

U.S. Oil Production, 1954–2007

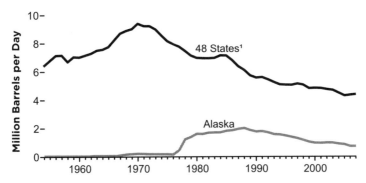

¹ United States excluding Alaska and Hawaii.

Crude oil production peaked in the 48 states at 9.4 million barrels per day in 1970. Alaska's production peaked at 2 million barrels per day in 1988. (Courtesy of U.S. Energy Information Administration)

The demand for oil continues to rise while the world's oil producers have begun to struggle to keep up with the demand, sending the prices to record highs. The Worldwatch Institute, an independent environmental research group in Washington, D.C., reported that oil production might not be able to meet the expected demand as early as the middle of the next decade.[9]

While America continues to need oil to run most of its infrastructure, other countries wait in line for it, too. Japan is the second-largest importer of oil in the world. China's development explosion has increased that giant country's demand for energy. The story is similar in other countries that are growing, Western-style, and whose leaders want the same quality of life Americans now expect. If they achieve it, the world won't be able to support the demand. Still, Americans use more oil, person for person, than any other nationality. We use a quarter of the world's oil and produce about 8 percent of it (even though our land contains only 2 to 3 percent of that supply).

Scientists began predicting the oil supply's peak and decline in the 1940s. M. King Hubbert, a geologist for Shell Oil Company, used his field knowledge to predict that American oil production would peak in 1970 and drop after then. That has come true. The Hubbert's Peak (or peak oil) referred to a bell curve he plotted estimating the height of production capability (based upon supply)—after which less oil would be found year after year, until the supply ran out. The United States hit its own "peak oil" production in the 1970s and has been producing less oil ever since, making up the difference with imports. The Alaskan pipeline slowed the drop in American production but did not reverse it; three-fourths of the oil in Prudhoe Bay has been pumped. The Arctic National Wildlife Refuge, a potential pumping ground long fought over in Congress, probably contains much less oil than the Alaskan pipeline. Oil production in the Gulf of Mexico has been declining since 1970.

Looking elsewhere around the world, peak oil was originally predicted to hit in 1995, but this did not take into account the Arab oil embargo of the 1970s. The latest guess is that the peak has happened, or it will happen sometime very soon in places like the Middle East.[10]

Oil certainly will not remain abundant and cheap past the next generation, and even if it hangs on a few decades after that, the trend toward scarcity won't reverse.

So far oil companies have proven themselves skillful at finding and extracting oil from sources previously considered marginal. ExxonMobil scientists "are developing technologies that are expanding the definition of recoverable resources," the company wrote in its 2007 annual report. "These innovations enable the commercial development of otherwise inaccessible or uneconomic hydrocarbons." From 2003 to 2007, unconventional sources made up much of ExxonMobil's 15.7 billion "oil equivalent barrels" of new sources of gas and fuel. About a quarter of these added sources was "tight gas," or natural gas trapped in sandstone reservoirs in the Rocky Mountains. ExxonMobil also is extracting heavy oil from oil sands, an enterprise not considered cost effective until recently, and pumping "deepwater" oil 3,900 feet down in the Atlantic Ocean 90 miles off the coast of Angola.[11] A potentially giant source of oil lies buried in shale—one hundred major deposits in the world include a large area in Colorado. The cost of extracting that oil, however, requires 1 Btu for every 3 Btu's of energy recovered. (A Btu is a standard of measurement I will mention several times in this book. One British thermal unit is the amount of heat needed to heat a pound of water 1°F at its maximum density of 39.1°F.) That cost could be too high to make this resource worth it. And that, too, would not last forever.[12]

The United States established a stockpile of emergency oil in 1975. The first deliveries began in 1977. The oil is stored in salt caverns on the Gulf of Mexico coast in Texas and Louisiana. The Strategic Petroleum Reserve (SPR) held about 670 million barrels as of late 2004. This is the largest emergency supply in the world. The Department of Energy explains that the country would dip into this supply during a "severe energy supply interruption" that they define as "of significant scope and duration" or a problem that "may cause major adverse impact on national safety or the national economy (including an oil price spike)" or an emergency due to "an interruption in the supply of imported petroleum products, or from sabotage or an act of God." The supply was tapped to ease shortages after Hurricane Katrina damaged refineries and portals on the Louisiana coast in 2005. When gas prices rose in 2008, the country halted deliveries.[13]

Unsettling.

The arguments in favor of oil remain largely economic. Even at record prices it remains an economical source for many things. But not for long. Taking the train or bus is starting to look good even in remote areas. But oil and its by-products, such as plastics and chemicals, do run the economy right now. Many political leaders focus on oil because, so far, there is still enough of it and it costs less to extract what's left than to invest time and money to bring alternative energy sources into the mainstream and create an infrastructure to support them. The U.S. government is studying alternative energy, but we remain far removed from an infrastructure that relies on it. We still look for oil. Meanwhile, everyday costs are rising dramatically, and the air quality is not improving, even with better ways of filtering smokestacks and car mufflers.

Natural gas

Natural gas is a mixture of carbon (about 75 percent), hydrogen, nitrogen, and a small amount of oxygen. Natural gas is transported in giant tankers in liquefied form. It arrives in houses via a system of about 250,000 miles of buried pipes. Natural-gas supplies are expected to last until between 2050 and about 2085.[14] We still rely on other countries for most of our natural gas. It's found in many places around the world, with most of it in the Middle East (more than 24 percent) and Russia (23 percent). North America holds more than 17 percent of the world's supply. Since September 11, 2001, the security risks of transporting huge tankers of liquefied natural gas and storing it in giant terminals on coastlines have emerged as a new problem.

It always comes back to the two concrete truths about all fossil fuels: We aren't making any more, and the climate is warming faster than at any time in the last century. Science is united on the cause of this acceleration: the human burning of fossil fuels. They pollute the air when burned, dirty the oceans when spilled, and, in the case of coal, create health hazards and scarred landscapes when mined. In spite of all this, people in many countries—particularly the United States—are using ever more power.

Starting in the late 1990s, power supplies couldn't meet the summer peak demands in California. Brownouts (reductions in the flow of electricity, making lights dim or flicker) became common and the threat of blackouts (total power outages) turned people's eyes toward the power grid. The power grid is the system of interconnected high-voltage lines in the United States (and parts of Canada) that carry power from power plants to locations where the power is needed. The term *grid* often includes the local distribution networks. There are more than six thousand power plants in the United States. The power from these plants travels on half of a million miles of high-voltage transmission lines. Their transmission to localized areas is handled through one hundred control centers where workers and automatic switching can direct the power to areas where it's most needed. Electricity funnels to local areas through substations, which "step down" the power to lower current. You have probably seen these jumbles of wires behind fences near your home.

Because the grid is interconnected, a lightning strike or a particularly high power demand from one region of the country can cut the power flow to other regions. Some of the major blackouts in history were started by one localized problem. The Northeast blackout of 1965 started when one line tripped in Ontario.[15] The August 14, 2003, blackout that left fifty million people without electricity in eight states and Ontario began with high demand and outages in Cleveland and Akron.[16]

Reading newspapers, listening to the radio, surfing the Web, checking out some of the new books, and watching television, I can't seem to get away from this problem of diminishing fossil fuel. That's good. A few years ago, no one talked much about it. Now the rising prices are the topic of the hour. Americans are starting to understand, to really get it: Unless a huge unfound reserve that's easily pumped shows up sometime in the next decade or so, people must figure out another way of producing electricity and heat.

Of course this isn't going to happen fast. It's going to take many decades. People will have to learn to think and act in new ways. This point can't be stressed enough: The alternative energy sources won't allow us to simply plug our energy-gobbling ways of life into new technology. We're going to have to learn to use less electricity and fuel than we have been enjoying for most of my forty-nine years, during which time the world population has doubled.

Thomas L. Friedman of the *New York Times* has written a new book on energy. I heard him speak at Brown University in April 2008, where two student activists threw green-colored cream pies at Friedman because he wasn't "green enough" for them. After he washed the banana-flavored green goop off his black turtleneck, Friedman calmly returned to the podium. He recounted the world pressures on energy supplies, particularly in the Middle East and China. He told his audience, "Everyone's going to have to pay the total cost of energy." He said we need three things: abundant, clean, cheap, reliable electrons; energy efficiency; and an ethic of conservation. "Without number three, that's a license to get a Hummer and drive it through the Amazon. . . . The scale of change we need is staggering."[17]

Author James Kunstler, a provocative yet gloomy critic of our wasteful oil-gobbling habits, calls the future "the Long Emergency."[18] While his words signal a warning I feel many of us need, I remain an optimist, and that's why I wrote this book. Several years ago a thoughtful businessman hired me to write an outline for a book I might ghostwrite about the state of the environment. At one point he turned to me and said, "You mean, you're optimistic for the future?" And I said, "Yes." Then he said, "Then, we can't work together." And so we didn't. I have two daughters. Anyone who has children believes in a long future for the planet, whether she or he thinks so or not. Humans want to live, and we have the intellects and personal energy to solve these problems.

Every now and then someone calls me a tree hugger, suggesting I am an emotional activist. I'm not. When I try to convince you that we are indeed going to have to change our ways, I do it as a citizen journalist. As a citizen, I want to say let's save energy now. As a journalist, I give you the information to move forward.

Highlights of the Energy Independence and Security Act of 2007

• **Better car mileage:** 35 miles per gallon for the combined fleet of cars and light trucks by model year 2020. The "corporate average fuel economy," or CAFE, will be funded by the repeal of two of the oil and gas tax incentives.

• **Ethanol production:** Whether from corn, cellulose, or other sources, the law sets a standard of nine billion gallons in 2008, increased to thirty-six billion gallons by 2022.

• **Lighting standards:** New standards for residential and commercial fixtures.

Incandescent lightbulbs are on the way out. The bill calls for the U.S. Department of Energy to run a contest for a solid-state replacement for the 60-watt incandescent lightbulb and for the PAR Type 38 halogen lightbulb. The goal is for the government to phase out incandescents and halogens within five years.

• **Appliances:** New efficiency standards for refrigerators, freezers, clothes washers, dishwashers, dehumidifiers, and other equipment.

• **Research funds:** Provided for green building demonstration projects, biofuels, electric car battery storage, electricity storage, and carbon capture and sequestration (the pumping of carbon emissions, particularly from coal, underground).

• **Not included in the act:** The two most controversial provisions of H.R. 6 that were not included in the enacted law were the proposed Renewable Energy Portfolio Standard (RPS) and most of the proposed tax provisions, which included repeal of tax subsidies for oil and gas and new incentives for energy efficiency and renewable energy.

Source: Fred Sissine, "Energy Independence and Security Act of 2007: A Summary of the Major Provisions," Congressional Research Service, December 21, 2007.

So much of the country's energy problem still circles around oil. We are not yet turning the entire country toward alternatives. It's natural to wonder why the country remains in the research stages when oil is running out and the environmental damage it's doing seems to worsen each year. Instead of trying to answer that difficult question, an ordinary citizen can ask a more practical question, to which there is an answer: What can I do?

When the average person looks at the big picture and doesn't see enough change unfolding, he or she can take action on the small level. Start at your house or apartment, and begin, step-by-step, to move away from fossil fuels. It's not practical to do this all at once, unless you are a millionaire. But within a several-year period, you can take steps to transform your house into a place that produces and conserves energy, rather than one that simply uses it and pays for it. Maybe you can't cut out all fossil-fuel use, but you can greatly diminish the amount you buy—and therefore contribute to cleaner air now and a better future. While you wait for political leaders to institute big policy changes favoring new energy sources, institute your own personal policy changes at home. If you don't make changes, history has shown us again and again that energy analysts will tell those leaders that the amount of energy we are using at home is what we "need," when my own experience proves otherwise. If my family can cut its energy use by a third in three years before making major changes, you can conserve and you can change. Make your own energy. Sell your power back to your leaders if you can—or if you want to. Take steps toward independence. It's the American way. The antidote to discouragement is action.

Americans and Energy

Net Electricity Generation: 4,053 billion kilowatt-hours

Residential-Bound Electricity Generation: 1,354 billion kilowatt-hours

Electricity End Use Consumption: 3,820 billion kilowatt-hours

Total Energy Consumption: 99.87 quadrillion British thermal units (Btu's), equaling 22.5 percent of world total energy consumption (Total energy consumption includes petroleum, dry natural gas, coal, net hydroelectric, nuclear, geothermal, solar, wind, wood, and waste electric power.)

Renewable Energy Consumption: 6.84 quadrillion Btu's, 2.9 quadrillion of which were conventional hydroelectric power (Renewable energy data from the International Energy Agency include hydropower, wood, biofuels, waste, geothermal, wind, and solar.)

Total Energy Production: 71 quadrillion Btu's
Total Energy Imports: 34 quadrillion Btu's

Energy Use, Expressed as Percentage of the Whole:
Residential: 21 percent
Transportation: 28 percent
Commercial: 18 percent
Industrial: 32 percent

Highway Transportation Fuel, Expressed as Percentage of the Whole:
Petroleum: 96 percent
Natural Gas: 4 percent

Fuel Share of Energy Consumption:
Oil: 40 percent
Coal: 23 percent
Natural Gas: 22 percent
Nuclear: 8 percent
Renewable Energy: 7 percent

Renewable Energy Breakdown:
Hydroelectric: 42 percent
Wood: 31 percent
Biofuels: 11 percent
Waste: 6 percent
Geothermal: 5 percent
Wind: 4 percent
Solar: 1 percent

Oil Consumption: 20.6 million barrels per day
U.S. Oil Production: 6.9 million barrels per day (crude and natural gas)
Oil Imports: 13.6 million barrels per day
Exports: 1.3 million barrels per day

Top Sources of U.S. Crude Oil Imports: Canada (2.3 million barrels per day); Mexico (1.7 million barrels per day); Saudi Arabia (1.5 million barrels per day); Venezuela (1.4 million barrels per day); Nigeria (1.1 million barrels per day), Iraq (0.6 million barrels per day); Angola (0.5 million barrels per day); Russia (0.4 million barrels per day)

Electricity Supply: (76 percent thermal-fired, 11 percent nuclear; 11 percent hydroelectric, and 2 percent "renewables").

Oil Pipelines: Around 2 million miles
Natural Gas Transmission Pipelines: 250,000 miles

Source: U.S. Department of Energy, Energy Information Administration; most figures from 2006.

Understanding oil supplies

"We pay more for water in the grocery store
than we pay for gas at the pump. . . ."
—*Roscoe G. Bartlett*

Searching for a smart plain talker on the problem of diminishing oil supplies—someone who does not work in the oil industry, in the alternative energy industry, for an environmental advocacy group, or for a lobbying firm—I settled on a member of Congress. U.S. Rep. Roscoe G. Bartlett is not the politician you would expect to tell the world that we must find alternatives to oil. He is a Republican, the party that rejected the Kyoto Protocol on limiting greenhouse gas emissions. He supports more domestic oil production. But his recurring message is that America must save energy and pursue renewable resources. Bartlett says energy is a nonpartisan problem and maintains a refreshing, almost naïve, approach about it, perhaps because he came late to politics. He is a sometime dairy farmer and former physiologist who invented oxygen recycling equipment for field use by pilots and rescue workers. He was first elected to Maryland's Sixth District in 1992.

In a speech he gave to a sparsely filled Congress on March 14, 2005, Bartlett, a consistent advocate for renewable energy, outlined world oil production and supply predictions and what he thinks the United States should do about them. He has given many speeches since then, but this one covered the problem succinctly. As many others have explained, Bartlett noted that in the 1940s, Hubbert, a geologist for the Shell Oil Company, tracked the pumping history of oil fields and noticed that each field produced oil slowly at first, then quickly offered up a lot of oil, after which it tailed off and failed to produce much. The fields' productivity records all followed a bell curve, Hubbert found. The top of the curve was when the field had produced half of its oil.

"Being a scientist, he theorized if you added up a lot of little bell curves, you would get one big bell curve, and if he could know the amount of reserves of oil in the United States—and he was doing this in the 1940s and early 1950s—and could project how much more might be found, he could then predict when the United States would peak in its oil production," Bartlett said.

In 2008, elected officials began to debate whether to lift a nearly three-decade-long ban on offshore oil drilling in many areas of the United States. Oil analysts and politicians have acknowledged it is not possible to know how much oil might be found if the ban were lifted, but it appears that, at best, it would be roughly a sixth to a fifth of U.S. production now—and that production is only half of what we import.[19] Bartlett also explained to the Congress that oil production in Alaska did not follow the bell curve, because first the pipeline had to be built and then the size of the pipe—four feet in diameter—limited the amount of oil that could flow through it. "We have pumped probably three-fourths of the oil in Prudhoe Bay," he said. "Debate has continued on whether to open up the Arctic National Wildlife Refuge [ANWR] for drilling. But ANWR has less oil than Prudhoe Bay."

Bartlett also reminded the House that oil exploration uses more sophisticated techniques such as 3D seismic detection. The oil geologists know where most of the oil in the world is located, and how difficult it might be to extract it.

"A couple of Congresses ago, I was privileged to chair the Energy Subcommittee on Science. One of the first things I wanted to do was to determine the dimensions of the problem," Bartlett said. "We held a couple of hearings and had the world experts in. Surprisingly, from the most pessimistic to the most optimistic, there was not much deviation in what the estimate is as to what the known reserves are out there. It is about 1,000 gigabarrels. That sounds like an awful lot of oil. But when you divide into that the amount of oil which we use, about 20 million barrels a day, and the amount of oil the rest of the world uses, about 60 million barrels a day, as a matter of fact, the total now is a bit over the 80 million that those two add up to. About 83 and a half, I think. If you divide that into the 1,000 gigabarrels, you come out at about forty years of oil remaining in the world."

As President Jimmy Carter noted during his administration in the late 1970s, up until that time, the United States had used as much oil in each decade as had been consumed in all of previous history. In other words, oil took over as a major energy source very, very quickly and accelerated startlingly.

Hubbert and Colin Campbell, an American scientist living in Scotland, predicted that the world production of oil would peak in about 1995—"without perturbations," as Bartlett explained it, adding, "But there were some perturbations. One of the perturbations was 1973, the Arab oil embargo. Other perturbations were the oil price shocks and a worldwide recession that reduced the demand for oil." Experts are debating whether the world's peak in oil production occurred in 2008.

Remember that all of this is still a theory, but that it appears to be a reasonably sound theory.

Bartlett was trying to make the nation think seriously about how long it would be profitable for companies to go after oil. Of course, so far oil company profits are very strong—but there is only so high a price can go before alternative energy begins to look more attractive. "How do we buy time, the time that we will need to make the transition to sustainability?" Bartlett asked. "Obviously, there are only two things that we can do to buy time. One is to conserve, and the other is to be more efficient." He added, "Remember several years ago when there were brownouts, blackouts in California and we were predicting, boy, the next year is really going to be rough? Do the members know why it was not and we did not see any headlines about blackouts in California? Because knowing that there was a problem, the Californians, without anybody telling them they had to, voluntarily reduced their electricity consumption by 11 percent. That is pretty significant. And that avoided the rolling blackouts or brownouts."

Bartlett remains somewhat unusual when he asks the country to make "major investments" in alternative energy. "This must ultimately lead to the ability to do everything within the capability of renewable resources," he said. "A few years ago, the largest buyer of solar panels in the world, and I do not know if that is true today, but a few years ago it was Saudi Arabia. Why would Saudi Arabia, with the most oil in the world, be the biggest purchaser of solar panels in the world? The reasons are very simple. These are not dumb people, and they figured out that solar panels were better for them in producing electricity than oil because they had widely distributed communities that were very small. Electrons in a wire are very different than oil in a pipeline."

CHAPTER TWO

Demystifying Solar Energy

In April 1977, in the midst of the energy crisis, President Jimmy Carter gave a speech beseeching the public to learn to get away from oil and promoting the need to conserve energy and find alternatives. Today his words sound eerily modern rather than nostalgic. Even though political leaders—especially city and state leaders—tell citizens to conserve energy at home, most of Carter's recommendations haven't happened. Now America finds itself vulnerable to oil-producing countries in the midst of Middle East unrest. Three decades later Carter's 1977 speech still lays out untested notions of dealing with energy shortages.

Here are the most memorable statements from Carter's speech:

> We must not be selfish or timid if we hope to have a decent world for our children and grandchildren.
>
> We simply must balance our demand for energy with our rapidly shrinking resources. By acting now, we can control our future instead of letting the future control us.
>
> Two days from now, I will present my energy proposals to the Congress. . . . Many of these proposals will be unpopular. Some will cause you to put up with inconveniences and to make sacrifices.
>
> The most important thing about these proposals is that the alternative may be a national catastrophe. Further delay can affect our strength and our power as a nation.

Our decision about energy will test the character of the American people and the ability of the President and the Congress to govern. This difficult effort will be the "moral equivalent of war"—except that we will be uniting our efforts to build and not destroy.

I know that some of you may doubt that we face real energy shortages. The 1973 gasoline lines are gone, and our homes are warm again. But our energy problem is worse tonight than it was in 1973 or a few weeks ago in the dead of winter. It is worse because more waste has occurred, and more time has passed by without our planning for the future. And it will get worse every day until we act.[1]

Three decades later, Carter's comparison of an energy revolution to a war strikes home, because we are in an actual war as I write this—a war that you could argue certainly involves protecting energy sources. How about an energy revolution that is like a war in all ways except it does not involve weapons and tanks and fear? How about a national crusade to reduce energy use on the way to changing energy sources over the coming decades?

To go solar, you must use less energy

When Carter went on to lay out the principles of his energy policy, he linked the growth of solar technology to learning to use less electricity. Without one, the other isn't possible. In the late 1970s, the country would begin to explore alternative energy technologies that could be produced at home. The cornerstone of the policy would be "to reduce the demand through conservation. Our emphasis on conservation is a clear difference between

In 1977, President Jimmy Carter said that using less energy would be "the moral equivalent of war." (Photo courtesy of Library of Congress, Prints and Photographs Division, U.S. News & World Report Magazine Collection, No. LC-DIG-ppmsca-09763)

this plan and others which merely encouraged crash production efforts. Conservation is the quickest, cheapest, most practical source of energy." Carter's words were rare for a leader, not because he asked each citizen to look inward and cut personal energy use (many presidents have said the same thing, with varying amounts of attention from the populace), but because he assumed that the country would have to brace itself for *not* finding enough oil to support the way we'd been living.

Two years later, in 1979, Carter tried to set an example when he ordered a solar-powered hot-water heating system placed on the roof of the White House staff kitchen. The government had to hire a contractor from Vermont to install the panels because no one in Washington knew how. The man spent that April installing 320 panels, each measuring four by eight feet, on the White House kitchen roof. The system heated some of the water for the staff kitchens, where several hundred employees ate.[2]

President Carter wanted solar energy to make up 20 percent of the country's power by 2000. But by 2004 the sun, combined with other alternative sources such as geothermal heat, made up less than 3 percent of the country's power.[3]

People who installed solar-powered systems in their houses during the Carter years received federal tax reductions. Americans spent $171 million on solar equipment in 1979. By 1981 they had spent almost $679 million (the government reimbursed up to 40 percent of their costs).

After Ronald Reagan became president in 1980, world markets and domestic attitudes changed. Oil prices dropped, and solar energy retreated. In 1981 Reagan's administration began to cut back on solar programs. In 1985 Carter's solar tax credits expired. Between July 1985 and July 1986, the price of home heating oil went from $1.04 a gallon to 66 cents. The number of solar equipment manufacturers dropped from about two hundred in the late 1970s to about thirty in 1985.

Sometime later Carter's White House panels stopped functioning. In 1986 a roof-repair crew took them down, and the White House announced they would not be put back. The news appeared in newspapers as an Associated Press brief, in which an unnamed government official said, "Putting them back up would be very unwise, based on cost."

The White House solar panels: relics of the dawn of modern conservation

For years after the Carter White House, the practice of gathering sunlight for domestic heat seemed to go the way of the crunchy granola eaters. From 1986 to 1991, Jimmy Carter's panels sat in a giant storage area in suburban Virginia. Then Peter Marbach, a development director trying to get Unity College in Maine some national attention, heard about the panels. He thought they were neither junk nor symbols of a mistaken energy policy. Marbach decided to buy the panels and put them to use at Unity College. "I just started making phone calls, and then I got the idea to write to Jimmy Carter and tell him what we were trying to do," said Marbach, who today is a photographer living in Oregon. "He wrote back amazingly fast. He sent back the letter I sent him and put a handwritten note on top: 'It would please me to see these panels restored. Good luck.'"

Marbach removed the seats from the school's basketball team's old bus, drove it down to Virginia, paid a few hundred dollars, and loaded the panels himself. When he got back, he raised money to install them. Even the most modern solar collectors for hot-water systems require some kind of a backup system to complete the job. Carter's vintage 1979 system only took the chill off water going into the oil-fired hot-water heater for Unity's meals, thereby cutting the fuel bill slightly. By doing only that, the panels did exactly what they were designed to do. For several years they did their job—until 1998, when a bad ice storm damaged the panels. For more than three years, they sat there. The physical plant director, Roger Duval, found a company in Portland that was willing to restore them for fourteen hundred dollars.

By 2005 Unity College had taken the panels off-line. They needed repairs. The college is trying to raise money and is interested in donating one of the panels to the Smithsonian and restoring the others as artifacts. And they are artifacts, but they also symbolize the hope of a technology that hasn't yet reached its potential. Marbach seemed an unlikely archaeologist when he rescued a piece of history. Perhaps heating systems like this

Jimmy Carter's solar panels on a Unity College roof. (Photo courtesy of Unity College)

do belong in museums—or perhaps not. Perhaps Marbach was just a master recycler. What he did do as he rescued the panels was to bring back into the public consciousness these solar energy artifacts that started out as symbols of hope and ended up as forgotten objects.

Carter believed that his solar panels would become common across the United States. The panels look like Cro-Magnon tools next to what we have today. But don't laugh at President Carter's panels. Instead salute the memory.

Solar technology: understanding the basics

Solar electricity is the quietest way to make energy. It is used primarily to heat water and generate electricity. To heat water, solar thermal collectors—which have improved greatly since the 1970s—employ pipes filled with solutions similar to antifreeze. The pipes run from the solar panels on the roof to a tank, where, submerged like coils, they warm the water. The earliest versions of these systems went up around the country beginning in 1973 in response to the first Arab oil embargo. These panels marked the birth of the modern solar industry. When another embargo pinched supplies in 1979, more solar companies formed. Between 1973 and 1979, the number of solar-collector manufacturers went from 45 to 225. The federal government, and many state governments, offered financial help for solar collector buyers.[4] Today's solar thermal collectors can pay for themselves in four

Source: U.S. Department of Energy, Energy Efficiency and Renewable Energy online fact sheets. See, www.eere.energy.gov/consumer.

These simple panels, affixed with liquid-filled pipes, heat some of the hot water for this Connecticut house. They have been in service for a quarter-century, proving that when owners care, these things can last. (Photo by C. M. Glover)

to eight years, according to the Worldwatch Institute.[5] In order to collect solar energy and convert it to electricity, a photovoltaic (PV) panel first absorbs sunlight into a semiconductor material, which could be a substance like silicon or cadmium telluride. The resulting electron activity is harnessed into energy through wires at the panel's back. The sun hits the solar PV panel, or module, each of which contains rows of cells—often thirty-six of them to a panel. (For an explanation of the physics of this, see "The physics of photovolaics" on page 41.)

The solar-collected energy travels down the wires to your fuse box and eventually to your lights and appliances, if you are using them. When you don't need the power, it goes into batteries (if you have batteries) that store the power until it's needed, or it goes through wires out to the street and to the regional power grid, if you are connected to a grid.

Whether or not the power is stored, the energy must flow through another box, the inverter, before it can power appliances and lights. The inverter converts the powerful direct current (DC) power to alternating current (AC) power, which runs everything electrical in the United States. Some appliances, if they are designed for it, can run directly off DC power collected in PV cells,

If your system stores electricity in batteries, the batteries can usually save a weeklong supply or more of power, depending on the size of the system. With today's solar PV systems, it's more common to tie the system in to the grid—since most rebate programs require this. When you tie into the grid, you do not store power unless you also invest in a battery bank. Grid-tied systems send unneeded power out of the house to electricity customers elsewhere. When excess power goes out to the grid, the meter runs backward. This usually happens in the middle of a sunny day, when few people are home. The utility company pays the homeowner for the power at wholesale rates. You won't get rich off selling sun power to the utility, but many people who do this have electric bills so low they seem caught in a time warp.

Practicality sets in

Only a few years ago, almost no one knew a solar-power user. That is starting to change. With not much fanfare, President George W. Bush's administration installed a set of solar photovoltaic panels on a National Park Service building on the White House grounds. While this move didn't grow out of Bush's personal appeal to the country in the way the first White House panels grew out of Carter's, the installation does prove that solar panels are simply too sensible not to use in such places. Look at highway message signs, portable construction equipment, and marker lights in your neighbor's garden and you will see solar PV panels. Look on the roof of the occasional house. Those mirrored rectangular panels aren't some strange decoration. They are solar collectors. Any ordinary person can begin to use them.

Production of solar equipment has grown quickly in the past few years. The Worldwatch Institute reports that worldwide production of PV cells increased by 51 percent in 2007, to 3,733 megawatts.[6] In 2007, the *Wall Street Journal* named First Solar of Phoenix the top-performing company. Founded in 1999, First Solar has made a name for itself by producing thin-film PVs that use cadmium telluride as a semiconductor instead of silicon, which has been in short supply in recent years. "First Solar's performance reflects bullish sentiment about renewable energy in general and solar technology in particular," wrote Rebecca Smith.[7]

The rebates arrive

Solar technology is on the rise, but it hasn't moved into the mainstream. Why? It all boils down to cost. PV systems are expensive, or about fifty thousand dollars for a system large enough to power a modest house. But a few years ago, many states began offering rebates that cover a good chunk of the cost of PV systems and solar-thermal systems. These rebates have made solar affordable to the middle class for the first time since the incentives of the Carter years (see the sidebar, "States Offering Financial Assistance to Buy Solar," on page 39).

Because solar is still a relatively new technology, and because it requires conservation, some people might feel reluctant to try it. But if a solar-photovoltaic system hooks into the power grid, backup power is always available. Still, solar users remain those rare individuals who are motivated to conserve energy. The solar users I have met talk about their conservation ethic. They don't want to have to resort to buying too much electricity from the grid—especially while they are still paying for the solar panels. They want to make it work. When they bought the panels, they also bought into a way of life. They made a commitment to spend more money than most to provide basic utilities, and every day they have to take steps to live differently at home—by using less power.

Many Americans pay little attention to the sun beyond its use for suntanning. Solar users have acted on their belief that the time has come when ordinary Americans need to look at the sun someplace other than at the beach. An artist I know in Old Saybrook, Connecticut, spent a year painting sunrises. One day he painted happened to be the first day of 2000. When he got to the shore of the Connecticut River, he found a crowd of people looking to the east, waiting with him for the sunrise. One of them suggested that after he finished his painting, he might like to take a drive around to a town beach on Long Island Sound, a few miles away. He headed over there to find a crowd of people patiently waiting for the sun to rise from the southwest. I can't scroll through a solar-photovoltaic company's online brochure without thinking how much so many people have to learn about the direction of the sun.

Getting started with solar

If you plan to harness energy from the abundant amount of sunshine that hits most regions of the Northern Hemisphere, be sure you know which direction is south. If your roof does not face the right direction, you can affix panels to poles set wherever they need to be. Then consider the funds. Does your state offer incentives or rebates? (See the sidebar, "States Offering Financial Assistance to Buy Solar" page 39.) Remember: In most cases, for every watt a solar panel generates, it costs roughly $8 to $10 in initial investment. Thus, 1,000 watts of power, or 1 kilowatt, would cost about $8,000 to $10,000. Generating 4 kilowatts, or enough to power a fairly conservation-savvy household, would cost roughly $32,000 to $40,000 to install the equipment.[8]

The average electricity use in my home state of Connecticut is about five times that amount, but people who go solar quickly get down to the lower level by incorporating major conservation moves into their habits (see chapters 8, 9, and 10). As of this writing, thirty states offer rebates for new solar-energy installations. The rebates cut the cost in half in my state, making a solar project a reachable goal for a middle-class property owner.

Beware: There are many signs around the country that solar rebates will not last. My state renewed its rebate program, but several of the leading states that have put out millions to help install solar systems have ended theirs. In New Jersey, which paid 70 percent of more than three thousand solar systems from 2000 to 2008, rebates ended in that year because the state said it would cost billions to reach its goal of providing just 2.2 percent of its power from solar by 2020. Officials are pursuing an energy-credit system instead. How this will help residential customers isn't clear, but New Jersey has been a big leader in solar energy, and it seems poised to try to do something. Other states looking into a different way of pursuing solar installations are New York, Colorado, and Maryland.[9] Whether this will move solar photovoltaics out of the affordable realm for ordinary people can't be known. Many states offer numerous incentives and credits for solar and other renewable projects, and these offerings change every few months (for details, see the Appendix). The systems eligible for rebates must tie into the electric-power grid so that any excess power drawn in can go out to the street lines to be used somewhere else. As long as the system provides 3 to 5 kilowatts a day, it will run backward during sunny times, when the household needs little power.

Starting small

I recommend considering small, appliance-by-appliance approaches to solar photovoltaics. Not only is it difficult to provide power for an entire household on the technology, you need not feel it's the only way to go. You can start very small, although to do so will feel like a hobby. It's possible to buy a single 100-watt panel for about several hundred dollars—but that doesn't include other equipment you need to hook up to the grid. (Remember: If you sign up to receive rebates or incentives, many of those

Solar panels in the tops of these lights illuminate a path after dark. (Photo courtesy of author)

programs require a grid connection.) Gail Burrington, owner of Burrington's Solar Edge in Windsor Locks, Connecticut, does not recommend that you go solar on such a small scale. According to Burrington, it would not be worth the cost to provide so little electricity for your house, but I think that even the exercise of working with a solar panel is worthwhile.[10]

The equipment is expensive. But so are cars, trips to Disney World, jewelry, houses, and cruise vacations—and all of those things don't reduce greenhouse gas emissions. It takes between fifteen and thirty years to recoup the financial cost of most systems—depending on the size of the system, electric rates, and whether a rebate covers part of the cost. But the environmental benefits begin immediately when you produce clean energy that doesn't pollute the air. Many objects for which we pay dearly depreciate from the moment we buy them. The Connecticut Clean Energy Fund explains in its guide for consumers that, "buying a PV system is like paying years of electric bills up front. You'll probably appreciate the reduction in your monthly electric bills, but the initial expense may be significant. Improved manufacturing has reduced the cost of PV equipment to less than 1 percent of what it was in the 1970s, but the cost amortized over the life of the system is still about 25 cents per kilowatt-hour. This cost is roughly twice the direct retail price that most Connecticut residents now pay for electricity from their utilities."[11]

One of the most inexpensive and sensible ways to light the edges of paths and driveways is the solar-powered driveway light. We have some that cost about $10 apiece at a home store, and at about $25 and up, you can buy sturdier ones that look quite nice.

If you dislike the look of solar PV panels on your roof, consider roofing shingles that double as solar panels. At least two companies produce these now. The downside is that they have been reported to be less efficient than the thicker PV panels.

Another way to start small is to invest in DC solar-powered appliances, each attached to individual solar panels that send DC to the appliance. (An inverter to convert to AC is not necessary, since these don't connect to the household electrical system.)

One of the most logical and useful solar-powered appliances is the solar-powered attic fan, also called an attic vent. It looks like a rectangular solar panel on the roof, but it includes a fan that blows hot air out of the house. The fan receives the most power from the solar unit when the house needs the fan the most—on hot, sunny days. These fans typically cost in the hundreds of dollars.

Or try a solar-powered sump pump, which doesn't rely on the electricity supply of the house that might shut down during a flood. Individual solar panels hook up to power laptop computers and other communication devices for field work or travel. Call any solar dealer to ask about these products, or search on the Web to learn more. DC solar appliances even turn up on eBay.

A solar system that would provide the amount of power most Americans use now would have to be very large—too large to be practical. Solar power in enough quantity can comfortably provide for needs, but it can't provide for the kind of waste Americans take for granted. So you would have to learn to turn off lights and power strips, unplug appliances that do not run off power strips, and stop using unnecessary electric appliances. Heating and cooling use the most energy. If you had a solar

A direct-current solar attic fan requires no hookup to any other system, doing its work most efficiently when the house needs cooling the most—when the sun is beating down. (Photo courtesy of Solatube International Inc. of Vista, California)

PV system, you'd need to heat your water with propane or a separate solar hot-water system. You'd also need to cut back on cooling. Start by buying a low-energy refrigerator. (Read about the history of conservation and tips for saving energy in chapters 8, 9, and 10.)

The Consortium for Advanced Residential Buildings (CARB), a program of the Department of Energy, has determined that energy savings from solar panels can vary greatly from house to house based on how carefully people conserve. In California in 2003, a construction company built a group of energy-efficient houses in Sacramento. The utility, Sacramento Municipal Utility District, offered solar systems to builders at a discount in order to encourage lower electricity usage. The built-in roof panels generated 3.3 kilowatt-hours,

Geoffrey and Joan Fitton provide electricity for their house in Old Lyme, Connecticut, with this solar photovoltaic array affixed to the roof of their attached garage. (Photo by C. M. Glover)

or theoretically enough to power the homes without backup power from the grid. The utility announced that the goal was for the houses to use zero net electricity throughout the year—in other words, to use only the sun. Throughout 2004 the utility kept track of electricity use at eleven of the houses. Only two of the houses reached the goal. The rest used varying amounts of added electricity above and beyond the solar systems. The discrepancies showed that "the ultimate responsibility in attaining 'zero energy' lies with the user," as CARB reported in a newsletter.[12] It's up to us to make this work.

One family's experience

In 2003 Peter Markow, a chemistry professor at St. Joseph's College in West Hartford, Connecticut, and his wife, Claire, decided to invest in a solar PV system for his house in Tolland, where they live with their son and daughter. They refinanced the house (this was before his state offered rebates) and located a clearing at the back of their property where they could mount the forty-eight 100-watt panels, which cost $51,000. "We have no real south-facing roof, so we mounted them on metal poles on concrete tubes going down four feet," he says. "We put them up in November 2003. In 2004, 81 percent of all our electricity needs came from the sun." As good as that was, he notes that the saleswoman had optimistically predicted that 100 percent of their needs would be fulfilled by the panels. It is true that occasionally, for short periods, the panels gave them much more than they needed. April 2005, for example, was an unusually sunny month with almost no rain. According to a computer program Peter monitors daily, the system provided 121 percent of the Markow family's electricity that month. (Of course the amount above 100 percent went out onto the power grid.)

Conserving electricity is not difficult, Markow says. They switched to compact fluorescent bulbs, which use much less energy than regular bulbs. The house is well insulated. They use an oil furnace. They close windows in the summer to keep the night's cool air inside the house. And the attic is insulated, holding in heat in the winter and cool air in the summer.

"I was doing this because I wanted to do it," he says. "I want to show the world that this is doable—right here in Connecticut." The truth is that solar PV panels operate better in cool temperatures, when electrons move off the silicon more efficiently.

Because the Markows made their move to solar without the benefit of government rebates, they would have to live well into their hundreds to recoup their financial investment in the panels. Connecticut has since instituted a rebate program that funds about half of the cost of most systems. Markow estimates that for the year 2004, they spent $50 on electric bills and generated power through the sun that would have cost them $550—for a net savings of $500 for one year. Markow doesn't care that their move to alternative energy isn't going to make them money. He didn't do it for the money, but the family found ways to make a sensible investment. They refinanced their mortgage from 7.7 percent to 5.5 percent and wrapped the solar cost into it. "The aspect I'd like to promote is: What's the environmental benefit of doing this, and the environmental *cost* of our energy use," Markow says. Using his computer program, which records the total amount of energy the panels bring in (whether it goes out to the grid or not), Markow is producing detailed records of his foray into alternative energy. (See chart on page 40.)[13]

States Offering Financial Assistance to Buy Solar

These states offer grants or loans to purchase solar photovoltaic systems or solar water-heating systems. For more details see the Appendix.

Arizona	Minnesota
California	Montana
Colorado	Nevada
Connecticut	New Jersey
Delaware	New York
Florida	Oregon
Georgia	Pennsylvania
Hawaii	Rhode Island
Idaho	South Carolina
Illinois	Texas
Louisiana	Utah
Maine	Vermont
Maryland	Washington
Massachusetts	Wisconsin
Michigan	Wyoming

The chart on the next page shows that the Markow family's 4-kilowatt solar array generates the majority of the electricity they need. Because this is a grid-connected system, when they calculate their costs and savings, they must consider the difference between what the power company pays them for excess power and what they must buy during dark or very cloudy periods.

Never forget that grid-tied solar systems do not store excess solar power at the house for later use. During the sunniest times of day, the power the house doesn't use immediately flows out to the power grid. After dark, any electricity they need flows in from the grid, and they must pay for that power.

This chart is based on the family's records in 2004, including the price of electricity at that time, which, including service charges, fluctuated between 13 cents and 14 cents per kilowatt-hour. Most months they spent slightly more for power than they saved by making their own, but as they learn to conserve at crucial times of the day, their savings could increase.

The State of Connecticut was not paying rebates when the Markows put in their system, but typically a system subsidized by a rebate will pay itself off in about twenty years. The Markows paid full freight for their system and acknowledge they won't pay it off. In most months, too, they paid out for more power than they took in.

Markow Family's Solar Electric Production and Savings

Month	Solar kilowatt-hours the Markows produced	Solar kilowatt-hours they used at home (the rest, they sold to the grid)	Power the Markows bought from Connecticut Light & Power, in kilowatt-hours	Amount they paid the power company	Money saved (Money spent)
January	379	104	397	$52.64	($10.69)
February	507	148	327	$44.89	$9.54
March	378	134	367	$49.32	($8.48)
April	495	152	324	$44.56	$8.60
May	506	144	265	$38.03	$12.86
June	478	164	292	$41.03	$10.71
July	451	259	452	$58.73	($8.81)
August	487	201	369	$49.54	$4.37
September	386	173	482	$62.05	($19.32)
October	353	112	335	$45.77	($6.58)
November	344	104	369	$49.54	($11.15)
December	273	97	477	$61.49	($31.16)
Total	**5037**	**1792**	**4456**	**$597.59**	**($50.11)**

Source: Peter Markow, who uses this chart in his classes at St. Joseph's College in West Hartford.

Don't think of this as a losing proposition, though. The Markows paid the power company only $597.59 for the whole year. If they had had to buy all of their power from the grid, that would have cost them more than $2,380.

Environmental Benefits of the Markow Family's Solar Photovoltaic System

Reduced Carbon Dioxide (CO2) Emissions
If burning #6 fuel oil: 92 gals saved x 20 lbs CO2/gal = 1,840 lbs
If burning coal: 188 lbs coal x 26 lbs CO2/lb = 4,888 lbs

Reduced Sulfur Dioxide (SO2) Emissions:
Acid Rain, Smog
If burning #6 fuel oil: 92 gals saved x 0.76 lbs SO2/gal = 7 lbs SO2

Reduced Nitrogen Oxides (NOx): Acid Rain, Smog
If burning #6 fuel oil: 92 gals saved x 0.053 lbs NOx/gal = 5 lbs NOx
If burning coal: 188 lbs x _ lbs NOx/lb = _____ lbs NOx

The physics of photovoltaics

Solar photovoltaics funnel energy through a semiconductor to wires. The way they work is rarely explained to the unknowing public. This description by my physics teacher husband, Nat Eddy, began as a discussion in the car, and I learned so much I decided to include it here.

Solar photovoltaic panels use light to produce electricity. They are generally made of silicon, which is a semiconductor. Semiconductors hang on to their electrons more tightly than electrical conductors like metals do, but less tightly than insulators. So under some circumstances they will conduct electricity, and under others they will not.

This is important, because the way they create an electrical current is that their electrons are held loosely enough that they can be knocked off when light falls on them (creating an area of positive charge), but held tightly enough that they do not migrate easily through the material to equalize the distribution of charges. This means that there is a potential (or voltage) difference between the front and the back of the silicon, and if a conductive path were made from front to back, current would flow to equalize the charges.

Silicon alone wouldn't be a very useful source of electrical current. The cells are not very efficient, so there aren't a whole lot of electrons being knocked off. So to be useful, photovoltaics must have a structure that allows them to produce and maintain a reasonably large voltage. Manufacturers "dope" the silicon, which means that they add to the silicon small amounts of other materials that have either more outer electrons, or fewer, than silicon has.

This means there is a source of extra electrons, or a lack of electrons (called holes), relative to the atoms of the silicon. The extra electrons can jump from atom to atom, and so can the holes, since when an electron from the silicon jumps into the hole, it creates a hole in the atom it left, which another electron can fill, and so on. So the doped silicon can conduct a current, by either electrons or holes being passed from atom to atom. If the doping provides extra electrons (which are negatively charged), it is called N-type, and if it provides holes (which means a missing electron, so the atom is positively charged), it is called P-type.

In a photovoltaic cell, a thin P-type layer is deposited on top of an N-type layer (or vice versa). Where the layers contact each other, the extra N-type electrons immediately fill in the holes in the P-type and neutralize or deplete each other. But deeper in the layers, away from the boundary, the charges—electrons and holes—attract each other. They migrate and cross over to the other layer. This means that the N-type layer becomes somewhat positively charged because holes have migrated over, and the P-type layer becomes negatively charged because electrons have migrated.

As the charges increase, the layers become less and less attractive to further charges, and eventually, migration ceases and equilibrium is established. Note that there is a potential difference between the layers, so a voltage has been established.

If light now falls on the photovoltaic cell, it will pass through the very thin P-type layer and knock off electrons from the N-type layer. It might seem that the electrons ought to jump into holes in the P-type layer, but remember—that layer has now become negatively charged, so instead, the electrons migrate away to the back of the N-type layer, where there is a metal backing. Electrons accumulate on the backing, creating a negative charge there.

Meanwhile, the holes created when the electrons were knocked off migrate to the negatively charged P layer. There, they diminish the negative charge on that layer, functionally creating a relative positive charge.

If the photovoltaic cell were not part of an electrical circuit, as the charges on the layers increased, it would become harder and harder for more electrons and holes to migrate, and equilibrium would again be established. But if the cell is made part of a circuit, the accumulated charges will be able to move off the cell through the circuit, and as long as light falls on the cell, electrons and holes will keep being created and migrating, maintaining a continuous potential (or voltage) difference, so that electric current will continue to flow.

And here endeth the physics lecture. Nat, I should point out, tells me he wishes he could have said more about this. But he's a science teacher. What would we do without them?

CHAPTER THREE

Wind Generators at Home

The first time I encountered wind power close-up was in fall 2003 in the White Mountains of New Hampshire, where I had just spent the night at the Galehead Hut, a backcountry cabin with bunks and meals. Walking outside in the morning, I heard a whirring, buzzing sound. I looked up and saw a tiny periscope-shaped object with a moving propeller perched on the roof peak. Its tiny propeller whirred so fast that it blurred as it collected energy to—it turned out—power the lights. The Appalachian Mountain Club, which operates these hikers' out-posts, uses clean energy wherever possible. From their perches at more than 3,500 feet above sea level, these wind turbines can collect enough power, along with solar photovoltaic (PV) panels, to run all of the hut lights. (The lights are turned off every night at 9:30 p.m. The extra power collected is stored in batteries.) Until you have seen a wind-gathering contraption, you might not appreciate the beauty of using a constant source of power. Get used to the idea. It's coming. Modern civilization had until recently ignored wind because petroleum has pro-vided the inexpensive lifeline.

You can use wind to make your home's electricity. You won't be able to power much of your house with the tiny ones, and they won't work well at the height of most rooftops in America unless, as one consultant told me, all you want is to power the brake lights of your car. Instead you will need a turbine with blades twenty feet in diameter that sit atop a very tall tower away from the house.

This basic technology isn't new, but until a few years ago the idea inspired little interest. In the 1970s a researcher described an already advanced wind-power technology in a textbook, noting, "Scarcely anyone has paid any real attention to the moral or ethical consideration involved in this, plus the next few generations burning up all the remaining fossil fuels and raising accumulated radioactivity far above the natural background level; many nations are now willing to at least discuss these things, but very little action has yet been taken." This researcher noted that a "mature" wind technology already was in place and that "assembly line production of components could start in a relatively short time. Wind power could impact the United States energy market starting in as few as four years if treated as a national priority goal." Of course, this did not happen.

The researcher was William E. Heronemus, a professor of civil engineering at the University of Massachusetts. Even he seemed ready for the public to reject wind when he noted that if people thought that wind generators looked ugly, then "they cannot be used." His remarks seem to have predicted the kind of reluctant fear that has greeted many large wind-farm proposals like the notorious fights over the Cape Wind project in the Atlantic Ocean off Nantucket Island. Energy Management Inc. won approval for 130 wind turbines designed to produce 420 megawatts of power, supposedly three-quarters of the energy needed on Cape Cod. The turbines would stand five miles offshore on Horseshoe Shoal, which is very shallow but usually submerged. Cape Wind's opponents, a well-funded organization of coastal residents like the Kennedys, showed how painful it is to make the transition to new, highly visible technologies—even among those who in other circumstances favor alternative energy.

In its infancy the wind-power industry has done better on a utility scale than on a backyard scale. The wind industry installed 5,244 megawatts of capacity in 2007, giving the United States an installed base of 16,818 megawatts in thirty-four states. The growth came as the latest federal tax credits were expiring.[1] The wind industry has historically grown and dipped in response to the ebb and flow of federal incentives for the fledgling industry. Harnessing wind for power goes back to the beginning of human history, with sailing ships. In the twelfth century, about ten thousand windmills ground grain and pumped water in western Europe. For most of the last century, though, windmills have remained a historic relic. Only a few years ago, residential wind power was not a household word. People tended to associate it with windmills in oil paintings of seventeenth-century Holland. Today most wind-power projects are large ones that send wind power through transmission lines from the windiest parts of the country, such as the Dakotas.

Wind power's undeniable environmental benefits butt against people's shock and resistance when they learn the height at which a wind turbine must turn in order to work. People who live near proposed wind farms here and abroad have protested the look of them. Most turbines are mounted on poles hundreds of feet tall. The reactions are explosive. In May 2005, for example, 350 residents of rural Highland County in western Virginia flocked to a hearing on the state's first proposed wind farm. A retired turkey farmer sought to build nineteen wind turbines, four hundred feet tall from base to top, on a ridge, generating 39 megawatts of power and more than $170,000 a year in tax revenues. Most of the county's residents signed a petition against the plan on the basis of how it would look.

Almost everyone who spoke that night was against it (one person called it "a crime against nature"), and the hearing went until 2:30 a.m.[2]

Blades from a wind turbine with other turbines in the distance. (Photo courtesy of author)

The individual wind-power gatherer faces fewer constraints. While utility-scale projects struggle to move forward, in many windy areas, residential-size projects aren't even a dream yet. Anyplace where enough wind blows, property owners may consider running their own power off a single wind generator. As with solar power, you can take steps now and buy a wind-power system. Beware, however: They are expensive and won't provide all the power you'll need—unless you have a lot of wind and enough room for a large unit. You must spend several thousand dollars for even the smallest of turbines. On the other hand, the payback time can be faster than solar if your turbine produces a lot of power. You don't have to wait for the country to sort out how to make wind technology mainstream. You can begin that transition at your place.

Necessary conditions for harnessing/collecting wind power

A house is ideal for an off-grid wind system if the wind in the area blows at an average annual speed of at least nine miles per hour. If your site is remote and would cost $15,000 or more per mile to connect to the grid, you're in an even better position. For a wind system that sells extra power back to the utility, the experts suggest that your annual wind speed reach at least ten miles per hour. High electric rates, rebates from the state, and friendly building codes, where available, help justify and reduce the dollars you'd spend. For instance, if you live in a place such as Southern California, where electricity rates are high, if the utility offers rebates (as California does), and if the building codes allow wind turbines, all of this can make the choice seem right almost immediately.

Energy experts suggest that you own about an acre of land so you can erect a wind tower away from your house and the neighbors. They also say that most residential wind customers must use larger turbines that sit atop tall towers at least sixty feet high. In order for wind to do the whole job for your house, you can't rely on one of those cute rooftop periscope-shaped turbines like the ones I saw in the White Mountains. Rooftop mini-generators must be in high-elevation locales, like the high-mountain huts in New Hampshire, or in ski huts in Colorado. Mick Sagrillo, a wind-energy consultant in Forestville, Wisconsin, with twenty-five years' experience, said of rooftop turbines:

"No. You don't put wind generators on your roof. These are toys." He explains that the principles of fluid dynamics dictate that the closer you are to the surface of Earth, the stronger the ground drag (or interference) is, which slows the prevailing wind speed. The greatest decrease in drag happens between the ground and sixty feet up. In an area with no trees, then, the turbine will work as it's designed to work at sixty feet. On land with trees, it must be thirty feet higher than the tops of the trees. You must know the tree heights, then add thirty feet, plus ten feet for the blades.

Above all you must live in a place where the wind generally blows steadily and strong. Wind power on the small scale is a great choice in windy parts of the country—and a dubious one in other places. If you live in North Dakota, South Dakota, Montana, Kansas, or Texas—the windiest places in the United States—consider using wind. The next fifteen windiest states after these, from windiest to least windy, are Nebraska, Wyoming, Oklahoma, Minnesota, Iowa, Colorado, New Mexico, Idaho, Michigan, New York, Illinois, California, Wisconsin, Maine, and Missouri.[3]

How they work

To the untrained eye, modern wind turbines look like gigantic propellers, with three thin blades designed to move faster than the speed of the wind. The blades are connected to a magnet generator that turns to make power. Like solar power, this energy starts out as direct current (DC) that is converted to alternating current (AC) through an inverter.[4]

When the wind blows, the three-blade rotors start turning. The faster the wind, the faster the rotors turn. The higher off the ground the rotor is, the faster the wind that turns it. The

Homeowners in mountainous Peshastin, Washington, make power from the wind with this Bergey Excel turbine, designed to generate 10 kilowatts under optimum conditions. It stands on a 100-foot-tall tower and is tied to the power grid. (Photo by Abigail Krich, National Renewable Energy Lab)

larger the blades, the more electricity they produce. The contraption automatically turns sideways in very high winds to avoid destruction; even then it still produces electricity. A typical roof model, producing perhaps 1 kilowatt of energy, measures 7.2 feet in diameter and begins turning when the wind reaches 6.7 miles per hour. A typical large pole-mounted turbine with three blades 8.2 feet long makes a rotor 16.4 feet in diameter, and the "swept area" is 211 square feet. The rotors on most turbines begin turning when the wind reaches about 7 miles per hour, although this can vary.[5]

Wind generators and the grid

In rural areas wind turbines may well operate off the power grid, but states that offer rebates require a grid connection. You should choose the connection that costs you the least. In areas with power lines near your house and state rebates, tying to the grid will cost the least. In remote locales, though, staying off the grid is cheaper than extending the lines to the house. On the grid, the wind power you collect runs your house until it exceeds what you need. When that happens, as it will on a very windy day or night, the power will automatically funnel out on the lines to the street lines. The meter will run backward, and the power company will pay you for the electricity. In a storm if the grid power cuts off, you have no backup energy stored at the house, even though you are hooked to the grid.

One couple's experience

In 2004 Becky and Phil Larson bought a house that came with a broken wind turbine in Elbert County, Colorado, east of Denver and Colorado Springs. "When Phil saw the turbine, he was just in awe," Becky told reporter Steve Raabe of the *Denver Post*. She insisted that they weren't "radical conservation freaks," but admitted that the turbine interested her, too.

They decided to rebuild it. They spent $8,000 and reduced their $400 monthly electric bill to about $200. They heat with electricity.[6] This move that seemed so unusual only a few years ago could become ever more common in regions like this.

Typical Prices for Wind Systems

The following chart compiled by wind consultant Mick Sagrillo shows the cost and output of several residential-size wind-turbine systems as of July 2008. Sagrillo says that many people are surprised to learn that the total cost—what he calls the "turnkey cost"—is considerably higher than the cost of the turbine and tower because of permits and the cost of construction.

Don't be too optimistic about producing the best estimates manufacturers make for your wind equipment. Companies calculate a "rated output" in kilowatts, but Sagrillo warns that the rated output is a poor measure of actual output because your own conditions affect its performance. Still it's a guide to the size of a turbine.

The first five machines (the Whisper 200 to the Whisper 500) are cabin-size machines designed for off-grid use. Of these tiny systems, only the Whisper 200 can be tied to the grid. The next six systems, from the Proven 2.5 through the XLS, are all small residential systems. The final three (V-1790-30 to PGE 20/32-30) are big residential systems. These produce more power than my house would need.

You can calculate how long it would take to pay off a system by dividing the kilowatt-hour output per month (choosing ten miles per hour, or twelve) by what you now pay per kilowatt-hour per month. The figure will show you the amount of money you will save per month using your system. Multiply that number by twelve months for your yearly savings.

Then you must add in the cost of operation and maintenance. Sagrillo says to put aside 1 percent of the total installed cost (in most cases) for a reasonable amount of money for yearly maintenance and for occasional new purchases of blades or bearings. Yearly maintenance always includes an inspection by the installer who will look for loose bolts and other problems.

In the chart, tower heights are followed by letters: T means tilt-up tower—a tower assembled on the ground and raised to a height such as the top of a building with a winch or a tractor. G means a guyed tower—one that is held in place by guy wires. F means freestanding tower.

Model	Swept Area	Rated Output	Typical Tower	Turnkey Installed Cost	kWh/year @ 10 mph	kWh/year @ 12 mph
Whisper 200	64	1 kW	84' T	$21,000	1,500	2,280
Proven 2.5	97	2.5 kW	105' T	$33,000	3,516	5,004
ARE 110	110	2.5 kW	105' T	$26,000	3,144	5,040
Skystream	115	1.8 kW	84' T	$19,000	2,880	4,560
Whisper 500	175	3 kW	105' T	$31,000	3,960	6,456
Endurance	254	5 kW	126' T	$45,000	4,587	8,068
Proven 6.0	254	6 kW	120' G	$62,000	8,004	12,996
BWC XL-S	415	10 kW	120' G	$60,000	6,240	10,800
ARE 442	442	10 kW	120' G	$71,000	14,052	21,972
Jacobs 31-20	754	20 kW	120' F	$77,000	19,728	32,292
Entegrity EW 15	1,902	50 kW	120' F	$190,000	50,000	88,000
V-15 35-1	1,964	35 kW	110' F	$150,000	43,000	64,000
V-17 90-3	2,462	90 kW	132' F	$190,000	62,520	101,640
PGE 20/32-1	3,120	35 kW	120' G	$260,000	56,234	79,893
PGE 20/32-3	3,120	50 kW	120' G	$260,000	70,811	105,918

©2008 Mick Sagrillo

Wind power facts

The wind industry is growing very fast, by about 30 percent a year in recent years, but provides only a small percentage of the total power in America—over 1 percent as of 2008 or 48 billion kilowatt-hours.

America provides about 17 percent of the global wind energy capacity.

The American Wind Energy Association says it is possible that wind could eventually produce 20 percent of America's electricity.

The wind in the United States could generate more electricity in fifteen years than all of Saudi Arabia's oil.

One wind turbine can provide $2,000 to $4,000 per year in income on farms, while using between 2 and 5 percent of the land.

Wind turbines must stand very tall to work. The three-blade rotors must turn at least thirty feet above anything that would stand in the way of the wind—such as trees or ridges.

Manufacturers often tout the peak energy output of their turbines, relying on hypothetical conditions. When comparing products, consider the blade size. The longer the blades, the larger the "swept area," or amount of wind collected.

The total installed wind capacity in the world, as of the end of 2004, was 47,317 megawatts, or roughly enough power for ten million households in the United States.

Sources: American Wind Energy Association; World Wind Energy Association.

CHAPTER FOUR

Other Technologies:
Fuel Cells, Biodiesel Fuel, and
Geothermal Heat Pumps

Researchers have described a world that runs on hydrogen (or a "hydrogen economy") for at least three decades. The descriptions so far read a little like a science fiction novel. The U.S. Department of Energy asks the public to picture a world where hydrogen filling stations are on every corner and where everything we can think of—from our cars to our laptops—potentially runs on hydrogen. Though this dream is not new, it has yet to come close to being true. What energy officials don't do is predict when this brave new world will arrive. Fuel cells will become important someday, but they will not be the new moon shot for America unless we find a way to power the larger ones without fossil fuels. Hydrogen fuel cells now power experimental cars and buses, provide electricity to equipment and appliances in remote locations and electricity and heat to office buildings and other institutions—including the Peabody Museum at Yale University. It appears, finally, that fuel cells indeed are moving forward to realize their huge potential in everyday use, at home, in cars, and in industry. Still, a lot has to happen.

Hydrogen fuel cells emit water vapor, although it's still not clear whether this is as benign a by-product as it seems.

Researchers have warned of another by-product of hydrogen fuel cells—the leakage of hydrogen. Researchers at the California Institute of Technology have estimated that leaked hydrogen in a hydrogen economy could decrease the stratospheric zone.[1] The other major problems to be resolved are 1.) establishing a new infrastructure to service and "refuel" hydrogen cars, 2.) avoiding the use of fossil fuels to build the cells, and 3.) perfecting the chemical reactions that create power in them.

Hydrogen, the most abundant element in the world, can be extracted from other elements, such as water, natural gas, and coal. Researchers would like to find a way to remove hydrogen from biomass—that large category of burnable waste products that come from plant, wood, and even animal and human waste. Natural gas is the most common hydrogen source. The necessary electricity for extracting hydrogen can come from traditional fossil-fuel-burning power plants or from wind turbines or solar photovoltaic cells that would link directly to the hydrogen production factory.[2]

In a fuel cell two oppositely charged metal plates surround an electrolyte. Hydrogen and oxygen atoms enter from different sides. The hydrogen is split into protons and electrons. Protons continue through the *anode* (one of the metal plates), and electrons are directed through the circuit to generate electric power. The protons and electrons then meet on the other side, where they combine with oxygen that has been passed through the *cathode* (the other metal plate), and combine to form the cell's waste product: water. Both the heat and water by-products of this reaction can be captured and used for other purposes.[3]

While this technology sounds almost perfect—a dream come true for the environment—one major problem with it is providing the energy in the cell that performs the chemical reaction.

For instance, two of the possible sources—or *feedstocks*—for hydrogen as a fuel are methane and water. In order to extract hydrogen from methane, you have to heat additional methane. In order to extract hydrogen from water, you have to provide electrical energy from a battery to begin a chain of events known as electrolysis of water. In electrolysis, water molecules break up into hydrogen bubbles and oxygen bubbles. The process of creating the hydrogen feedstock for fuel cells is not very efficient unless the hydrogen can be extracted without burning fossil fuels. If you must use fossil fuel to extract the hydrogen, the heating value of the hydrogen from the cell will be less than one-third of the heating value of the fuel burned in a power plant to extract the hydrogen.[4]

Hydrogen fuel cells to heat the home aren't available yet. Some companies and countries are working in earnest to make hydrogen the next major fuel. The challenge is going to be providing an infrastructure for hydrogen availability and production. For a few years now California has been funding initiatives to build hydrogen fuel stations for its "Hydrogen Highway" initiative.[5] (For more information on this, see chapter 7.)

One company has moved ahead with a self-contained fuel cell available for purchase. SFC Smart Fuel Cell AG of Munich, Germany, founded in 2000, went public in 2007 to advance its methanol-driven fuel cell designed for use in remote areas. It weighs about fourteen pounds. Using a liquid fuel in cartridges solves the problem of a lack of fueling infrastructure, says Peter Podesser, the company's CEO. "What we have done here is a selection of early markets where the customer benefit of this technology is higher than the price sensitivity." Their cell has found a niche at remote flood-watch stations, in remote camera systems, with the military, and in off-grid cabins and recreational vehicles.[6] Wartsila, a power company in Finland, provided electricity for a month long fair in Vaasa, using a fuel-cell power plant run on waste methane from the local landfill. Radian, Inc., of Alexandria, Virginia, and a Canadian company, Hydrogenics Corporation of Mississauga, Ontario, signed a contract in 2005 to manufacture a fuel-cell system for the Stryker, a U.S. Army light-armored vehicle, or LAV. It would use a proton-exchange membrane fuel cell and provide the hydrogen using electrolysis.[7] In Flint, Michigan, Kettering University and the city's transit authority put five fuel-cell minibuses on the streets in October 2007.[8] Iceland announced in 1999 that it would become the world's first hydrogen economy, and its leaders are working with major corporations such as Shell Hydrogen, DaimlerChrysler, and Norsk Hydro to convert Iceland's transportation sector to hydrogen over the next thirty to forty years, as Seth Dunn reported in a Worldwatch Institute paper in 2001. The first fuel-cell buses began driving in Iceland in 2002.

The fuel cell that powers this Mercedes-Benz Citaro city bus is located in its roof. (Photo courtesy of DaimlerChrysler)

Dunn says that the impact of a move to hydrogen on the economy "will be staggering, putting the $2 trillion energy industry through its greatest tumult since the early days of Standard Oil and Rockefeller." Many companies are developing fuel cells to perform a huge range of tasks that would indeed make them as ubiquitous as electricity, if the plans come to be. Fuel cells would run cell phones and laptops, vending machines, houses and institutional buildings, cars, and planes.[9] Some companies are testing small fuel-cell systems that would generate from 3 to 10 kilowatts of power for houses. The expectation is that this electricity would be cheaper than what we can get today. Fuel cells have already been tried in hospitals and computer centers worldwide.[10] Micro fuel cells, to replace batteries, could someday power laptops, telephones, and portable generators.[11]

All but the skeptics—and there are some skeptics—believe that hydrogen fuel cells will mark a chapter in energy history as significant as the era when coal ruled, in the eighteenth and nineteenth centuries, or when oil took over, in the twentieth century. Worldwatch warns that the United States could lose its status as a superpower if it does not move to hydrogen technology soon. "Countries that focus their efforts on producing oil until the resource is gone will be left behind in the rush for tomorrow's prize," the Worldwatch authors wrote. "As Don Huberts, CEO of Shell Hydrogen, has noted: 'The Stone Age did not end because we ran out of stones, and the oil age will not end because we run out of oil.'"[12]

One of the most public of the skeptics, James Howard Kunstler, would not agree with these predictions. "The widely touted 'hydrogen economy' is a particularly cruel hoax," he writes in his 2005 book, *The Long Emergency*. "We are not going to replace the U.S. automobile and truck fleet with vehicles run on fuel cells. For one thing, the current generation of fuel cells is largely designed to run on hydrogen obtained from natural gas. The other way to get hydrogen in the quantities wished for would be electrolysis of water using power from hundreds of nuclear plants. Apart from the dim prospect of our building that many nuclear plants soon enough, there are also numerous severe problems with hydrogen's nature as an element that present forbidding obstacles to its use as a replacement for oil and gas, especially in storage and transport."[13]

For a professional coalition of fuel-cell manufacturers, the World Fuel Cell Council, the conversion is happening too slowly. The council has said that the public does not fully support the new technology, so costs are still high and few products have gone on the market. The council believes that city buses (tested since the 1990s) will provide the first major place for the new technology. "Hydrogen fuel-cell buses are now sufficiently technically advanced to enter the market, but extensive field demonstration and fleet testing is required to prove performance and build confidence in the technology," the council writes.[14]

Honda introduced a new fuel-cell car on June 6, 2008. The first lucky owners were from California, where about forty hydrogen filling stations exist. Honda's marketing staffer Jim Ellis told National Public Radio's *Science Friday* that the car could drive from Los Angeles to Las Vegas with one fueling stop midway.[15] So, it is happening.

A Mercedes fuel-cell car tested in 1999 is twice as energy efficient as a diesel version of the car—but the liquid hydrogen tank allows the car to go only 280 miles before refueling. Other major car makers such as DaimlerChrysler, GM, Ford, Toyota, and Nissan aim to sell hydrogen cars soon. Journalist Jim Motavalli test-drove a fuel-cell car in 2005 and reported that it worked quite well.[16] (For more on cars, see chapter 7.)

Honda introduced a new fuel-cell car in 2008. The first lucky owners live in California, where hydrogen filling stations have opened. (Photo courtesy of Honda)

Fuel Cells Are No Modern Phenomenon

The history of fuel-cell studies shows that the challenge has always been to devise a practical and inexpensive fuel cell. It all started in the nineteenth century.

A Welsh scientist named William Robert Grove developed a wet-cell battery in 1838. It generated about 12 amps of current. Scientists argued over still-developing chemical theories that would explain how current could flow in Grove's battery. In 1893 Friedrich Wilhelm Ostwald further explored the chemistry of Grove's fuel cell.

For years there emerged no practical applications of the fuel cell that would enable it to replace other fuels. European scientists continued to work on fuel cells. In 1889 Ludwig Mond and Carl Langer extracted hydrogen gas from coal and were able to generate 6 amps per square foot at 0.73 volts.

Meanwhile, two other scientists struggled with a similar fuel cell, complaining that gases leaked from one chamber to another. These two, Charles R. Alder Wright and C. Thompson, said that if the cost were no object, fuel cells could be built with large enough coated plates to allow enough current to be created. Others also believed that the cost was too high or that the savings to consumers were not high enough. William W. Jacques released his so-called carbon battery, which also used coal, in 1896. His battery, which made power with a thermoelectric action, turned out to be terribly inefficient.

Swiss scientist Emil Baur studied fuel cells in the early twentieth century using such materials as molten silver, clay, and metal oxides. O.K. Davtyan of the Soviet Union experimented with other materials.

Francis Thomas Bacon of Britain began studying electrolyte fuel cells in the late 1930s. He put aside his research during World War II. By the 1950s he had developed expensive but relatively efficient fuel cells using potassium hydroxide instead of acid electrolytes. Pratt & Whitney licensed this technology for spacecraft.

A Canadian engineer, Geoffrey Ballard, developed a proton-exchange membrane in the 1980s. This created the chemical reaction necessary but at low temperatures. He began testing fuel cells in vehicles. In the 1990s, Daimler Benz (later DaimlerChrysler) developed a compact Mercedes that could go 280 miles on one tank of liquid hydrogen.

Source: Smithsonian Institution (see its lengthy and helpful Web page on fuel cell history at http://americanhistory.si.edu/fuelcells and www.whyfiles.org)

Biodiesel fuel

The original diesel engine, invented by Rudolph Diesel in 1900, ran on peanut oil. Peanut oil and any vegetable oil can be refined to run automobile engines or furnaces. Since 1998 the federal government has counted biodiesel fuel as an alternative fuel, leading to an increase in the number of biodiesel users seeking

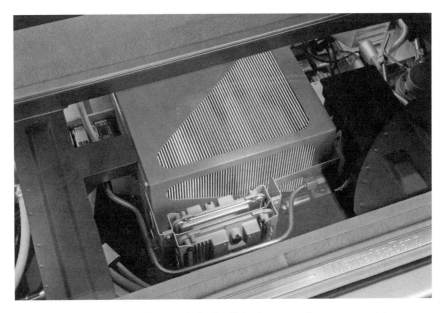

In this cutaway view of the car's fuel cell, hydrogen and oxygen react to produce water, creating electrical energy. (Photo courtesy of DaimlerChrysler)

a federal tax credit. The U.S. Postal Service and the U.S. Departments of Defense, Energy, and Agriculture use the fuel in their vehicles. The fuels are starting to run buses, vans, and garbage trucks.

The tax credit is one penny per percent of biodiesel in a fuel blend made from vegetable oils and one-half penny per percent for recycled oils. This incentive is taken by petroleum distributors and passed on to consumers. The United States Department of Agriculture (USDA) has predicted that the demand for biodiesel will continue to rise. If petroleum prices continue to escalate, biodiesel could become a bargain. Much of the biodiesel sold commercially today is made of soybean oil. It's available only in limited areas. It takes about 7.3 pounds of soybean oil, which costs about 20 cents per pound, to produce a gallon of biodiesel. Biodiesel costs at least $1.50 per gallon to produce. Used restaurant oils can produce fuel for as low as $1.00 per gallon.[17]

Some biodiesel users refine the fuel at home. Their experience illustrates the simplicity of the process. This chemical reaction can go on inside an old hot-water heater perched in a garage or barn. The resulting fuel can either be mixed with Number 2 heating oil to make your heating furnace burn more cleanly or used on its own in furnaces or vehicles. Biodiesel fuel reduces hydrocarbon and particulate emissions by more than half. If you use a mixture of 20 percent biodiesel and 80 percent fuel oil, you reduce emissions by up to 20 percent, according to *Mother Earth News.*[18]

How could people not have tried this sooner? Well, oil was so inexpensive until recently that most people wouldn't have bothered. Nevin E. Christensen, a Connecticut egg farmer and operator of a petting zoo, is now bothering. He has started making his own biodiesel in a shed. He uses the fuel to power his tractor. He starts with two hundred liters of "old gunky waste veggie oil from restaurants," which he pumps into an abandoned eighty-five-gallon water tank. He heats the tank to 130°F. In a separate tub, he mixes ten gallons of methanol and three pounds of household lye (such as a product you'd use to unclog your drains). He pumps this by tube into the heated vegetable oil and mixes it for half an hour, then shuts it off. The glycerin in the oil settles out to the bottom. He removes it to run through old nylon stockings to make soap, the old-fashioned way. The remaining liquid in the tank is his tractor fuel.

"I never thought I could do something like this," he says. At first he was scared when filling the tank. Vegetable fuel gives off no black puffs of particulates, as petroleum-based diesel does. The tailpipe smells like french fries. Vegetable-based biodiesel burns 75 percent cleaner for all pollutants except nitrous oxides, he says. "We could grow 25 percent of our diesel fuel on land, now fallow, which the government paid us not to use."[19]

Biodiesel excites people who try to save energy at the individual level because in many cases it makes use of locally available oil that would have otherwise been discarded, or oil derived from plants that grow domestically. Another energy source lying quietly in wait is even more local than biodiesel, and also has entered the ordinary person's green lexicon: that is, the constant air temperature a few feet below the surface of anyone's yard. Read on to learn how to tap into this source that until recently many people weren't thinking about.

Geothermal heat pumps

The temperature six feet below the soil stays relatively constant, even in frigid climates, ranging from 50°F in the North to 70°F in the South. Geothermal heat systems circulate water or anti-freeze through several hundred feet of pipes, called a loop, bur-ied in the ground or submerged in a pond or lake. These tubes of fluid can serve either for heat gathering or heat dispensing, depending on the season. In winter the system concentrates the earth's natural heat in the fluid and circulates it back into the house, and, then, using electrically driven compressors (sort of like an air-conditioner in reverse) and heat exchangers, it raises the fluid's temperature to 100°F or more, which can then be used to blow hot air through a house's duct system or can be pumped through a radiant floor heating system. Geothermal heat pumps generally cannot raise the water temperature high enough to be used directly in baseboard or radiator systems.

In summer the heat pump works in reverse, drawing warm air out of the house. Systems can be rigged with a component that will loop into the hot-water tank. This works best in the summer when there is extra heat to be had.

Two types of loop systems are used, depending on the size of the house's yard or property. Horizontal loops are used when the homeowner has a yard large enough to bury hundreds of feet of tubing parallel to the surface of the ground. For small yards a vertical system can be used, where pipes descend 150 to 450 feet into the ground.

Geothermal heat can be captured from the Earth in either horizontal (opposite) or vertical (above) loops of pipe.

Horizontal geothermal heat system.

You must calculate the cost of installation, the electricity spent to circulate the fluid in the loops, and the electricity the heat pump compressor uses to bring the water temperature up to 100°F. But it will almost certainly save a household a lot of power. Depending on pump size and house size, you can save 30 percent to 40 percent of the cost of conventional heating systems.

Heat pumps will cost you about $2,500 per "ton" of capacity, a commonly used measure. An average house uses a three-ton unit costing about $7,500 (this doesn't count installation; more on that below). This is a bit more than the initial cost of a traditional heating and air-conditioning system, though, of course, the energy savings begin to mount from the time you buy your geothermal heat pump. If you finance the heat pump with a special loan (known as the energy-efficient mortgage), you can build the payback into a low-interest (one hopes) loan payment. A good system will pay for itself in energy savings in between two and ten years, and the pumps last for twenty-five to fifty years.[20]

The one aspect of geothermal systems that makes me uncomfortable is how difficult it is to find information about it. We know from industry brochures and brief explanations from various sources that, once they are installed, geothermal systems will save power. But the equipment and installation costs can be considerable. One Connecticut resident, George Goodrich, told me he was quoted $30,000 to $36,000 for installation of a geothermal heat pump for his 1,500-square-foot house. Although geothermal requires very little outside power to operate, that is another factor to consider. So are the quirks of your property. Goodrich's house is all one level, with a mechanical room in lieu of a basement, and the geothermal loop was to be buried in a vertical well (see illustration on page 66). But Goodrich said he decided on a pellet stove instead because of the considerable up-front cost of the geothermal heat pump. One contractor told him he would need to hold onto his oil furnace as a backup, and another one told him he wouldn't; the heat transfer was going to be via 20 yards of ceiling pipes, and so Goodrich was leery.[21]

Joel Gordes, who's been an independent energy consultant for three decades in West Hartford, Connecticut, said that geothermal systems usually cost in the $20,000 range. "When the ground source heat pump first came out, the Electric Power Research Institute (this was the mid 1980s) suggested that it was good for drafty old farmhouses and large houses that were not easy to insulate," Gordes says. For a superinsulated house that doesn't need much heating, geothermal savings won't be as dramatic. "Let's say that house uses the equivalent of two hundred gallons of oil, and let's say you have a house the same size, but it's a drafty old farmhouse and uses the equivalent of two thousand gallons of oil. Let's say the heat pump saves you 30 to 50 percent [in energy costs over your old system]. That's going to save you about one hundred gallons of oil a year for the superinsulated house, but the house that uses two thousand gallons a year, the 50 percent savings is going to be one thousand gallons."[22]

Geothermal systems are big projects that should be undertaken carefully. On the right property, they make sense. Gordes advises people to find independent experts to help them navigate the choices. "When you start making big decisions like this, everyone should go to an engineer who is capable of coming up with a heat-loss analysis. There are going to be a lot of people out there promising you, 'It's going to do this, that, and the other thing.' Go to an engineer who doesn't sell a product—someone who's in sole practice, a consulting [mechanical] engineer."[23]

CHAPTER FIVE

Heating with Wood

In North America people love heating with wood. But lately there are reasons enough to feel guilty about it. We feel guilty using wood because fireplace fires draw heat out of the house while warming a tiny area. We feel bad because even though woodstoves heat efficiently, they—like fireplace fires—pollute the air. But woodstoves have been improved: The smoke that comes from newer stoves is much cleaner than those made before the 1990s—as long as you maintain the stove. So none of these reasons should stop you from substituting wood for some oil, natural gas, or electricity to heat part of your dwelling. Yes, you must pay attention to the problems wood can cause if not burned properly or in the right kind of stove. That aside, clinging to many of the bad feelings that circulate about wood burning is, in my opinion, a useless exercise—on par with feeling bad because we use any resources at all.

Woodstoves aren't the only home-heating method that pollutes. Almost every form of heating a house or apartment pollutes the air—especially because we're more inclined to crank up the heat with these systems than we are with a woodstove, which requires hand-feeding. Woodstoves may have gotten a worse reputation than oil-burning home furnaces, which are much more common.

Still, the pollution from woodstoves is real—and it can be worse if you neglect the stove. Government scientists have labeled woodstoves as major polluters because they emit microscopic burned matter known as *particulates*. This pollution includes polycyclic organic matter (POM), a large group of particulates formed from burning a long list of substances from steak on a grill to cigarettes to wood to automobile fuel. Seven of the POMs are classified as cancer-causing agents. Animals who inhaled one category of POMs in a lab setting developed tumors and leukemia.[1]

It is not difficult to understand why the government requires new woodstoves to filter out many of the particulates. The rules are part of "new source performance standards" of the U.S. Environmental Protection Agency (EPA). Manufacturers outfit new stoves with afterburners that ensure that particulates and carbon burn almost completely before the smoke goes up the chimney. These stoves won't continue to burn cleanly after the first few years if owners don't clean them and keep the filtering components in working order. Catalytic converters as afterburners have largely fallen out of favor, because after several years you have to pay a few hundred dollars to install a new one. It seems a good bet that stove owners will get a little lazy with maintenance. When the EPA evaluated sixteen of the newer stoves in Oregon over forty-three weeks in the late 1990s, they found that cleaner stoves lost efficiency in filtering out particulates when they were only a few years old. Even so, "on average, after about seven years [the stoves] still have lower emissions than uncertified conventional stoves."[2]

It's within the power of an individual to burn wood cleanly in a newer stove that's properly cleaned and maintained. This is a better step toward improving air quality than unspecified guilt over large utilities' emissions. Older coal- and oil-burning power plants in the United States operate without having to upgrade to newer technology. So dare to enjoy a woodstove, which provides an affordable source of heat—especially if you can cut your own wood. And dare to feel proud that if you use a new stove, you're taking further steps than many power plants. Of course we won't be arrested if we use older stoves. This is a voluntary program. Finally, feel glad that you are reducing the amount of oil, coal, electricity, or natural gas you would otherwise burn for heat in your house.

The reasons we love wood fires go deep into our primitive psyches. It isn't just that we love to sit around crackling logs. It's because wood fires built civilization in many parts of the world. Wood is a local fuel source for those who live in forested regions. It stands or lies ready on the ground (whether we gathered it up ourselves or not). It lights quickly and is easily put out. You control when the heat begins and when it ends.

Before 1900, 90 percent of Americans burned wood for heat, but as coal came into wide use, followed by oil, wood became unpopular except to produce ambience. By 1970 only 1 percent of the population heated with wood.[3] After the energy crisis of the late 1970s, homeowners started burning wood again and there was a mini stove boom. In the 1980s woodstoves fell out of favor because of the particulate pollution they emitted, and the federal government enacted stricter controls. This led to major improvements in stoves beginning in 1985; woodstove manufacturers devised stoves that could cut the amount of nitrogen oxides, carbon monoxide, and particulates. Today's woodstoves burn cleaner than anything pre-1990.

Despite all this, burning wood does create particulate pollution, and anyone using wood for a fuel should do everything possible to reduce the pollution. The new stoves ensure that the least amount of pollution possible reaches the air. Woodstoves made after July 1, 1988, were required to meet pollution-filtering standards set by the EPA. Two years later, in 1990, more stringent Phase II regulations went into effect. The new standards require new stoves with catalytic converters to emit less than 4.1 grams of particulate matter per hour. Stoves without catalytic converters must emit no more than 7.5 grams per hour.[4]

Critics say that even cleaner-burning stoves can't change the fact that wood still pollutes. That is true, but not in the sense that burning oil and coal pollutes. Those who champion wood for heat note that the carbon released during wood burning is the same amount that the wood would release if the tree were to fall to the ground and rot.[5] Coal, oil, and gas also release carbon when they burn, but these releases come from very old stores of energy that are burning now only because people have gone to the trouble to drill for them. Releasing that much carbon into the air over a few decades' time has altered our world.

Don't fall for the other argument (dating to President Reagan's famous, although not unique, comment that trees cause pollution), which asserts that trees and plants naturally pollute more than cars or factories do. This is a skewed way of considering the fact that plants put more carbon dioxide into the atmosphere than burning fossil fuel does. Yet plants are supposed to put carbon back into the atmosphere after they take it up. It is the burning of fossil fuels like oil and coal—which is not part of a natural cycle—that has led to our current situation. Burning fossil fuels alters the natural carbon cycle. People can't change the amount of carbon dioxide coming from trees. It will be the same whether the wood is burned in a stove or rots on the forest floor. We can change greenhouse-gas emissions by refraining from burning fossil fuels. These emissions would not exist without human beings.[6]

Outdoor wood furnaces

One type of wood furnace is gaining popularity—the outdoor wood furnace. It offers both benefits and potential problems, according to Dirk Thomas, a chimney sweep in Vermont and author of *The Wood Burner's Companion*.[7] The benefits include that the wood fire burns away from the house, eliminating smoke, ashes, and inconvenience. Asthma and respiratory disease sufferers benefit. The downside is that many outdoor furnaces are quite large and can burn smoky fires. Many models are equipped with automatic shutdowns to prevent them from overheating the water in the boilers (which provide heat to the house).

Outdoor wood-burning furnaces, or boilers, can heat an entire house, along with hot water systems, swimming pools, and more. They're best used in a rural setting, where the smoke won't bother neighbors. (Aqua-Therm wood furnace installed by Pete Mostehrt of Delhi, New York)

If you live in the suburbs or city, where your neighbors are close, an outdoor wood furnace is not the best choice, because the chimney is low enough for smoke to be bothersome to neighbors. But in rural areas they make a lot of sense. Be wise about the fire: Use dry wood, don't throw in trash or green stumps and, of course, maintain the unit. And finally, place the outdoor furnace where the prevailing winds won't bring the smoke into your house.

If your wood source is free, and you are hardy enough to split and feed the fire twice a day, an outdoor wood-burning furnace is a good plan. If oil prices stay high, the furnace can pay for itself in about four years.

The hearth

For simplicity and ambience, not to mention flexibility, a wood-stove provides an excellent source of heat, particularly as a backup to a furnace. If you spend most of your time in your house and don't mind tending a stove, a woodstove can provide most or all of a small house's heat, as long as the stove is centrally located and the fire properly tended with good, dry wood.

Buy newer stoves and maintain them

In order to responsibly heat with wood, stove owners must take care of their investment. Each year my fuel-oil company calls and insists that we allow them to come to the house to clean the furnace. A woodstove owner must think in the same way. Call the chimney sweep each year. Check with the stove dealer on other routine work the stove needs. Be responsible, and the stove will do the same.

Dan Melcon, a woodstove seller, says it's not fair that wood-stoves have gotten a bad reputation since the late 1980s. Millions of old stoves are still out there, though, and he warned that people should replace them soon. "The analogy I use is that it's as if people were continuing to use computers from the early 1980s," he says. Of course many of those old stoves sit unused in the corner while people turn up the thermostat, as Melcon put it. So invest in a newer stove and take the old one to the metal pile for recycling. The air will benefit.[8]

A Vermont Castings woodstove in action. (Photo courtesy of Lilly Golden)

Is there enough wood?

What if heating with wood were to take off in popularity and most people wanted to do it? Would Americans burn down all the surplus firewood in a few years? It seems highly unlikely. As attractive as wood burning might be when considering the alternatives, using woodstoves will interest only those people willing to do a little work to build fires; cut, stack, and carry wood; and sweep up the ashes. For this population there is more than enough wood.

Forester Stephen Broderick of the University of Connecticut Cooperative Extension has studied wood supplies for burning for two decades and burns wood at his house. He says, "We grow significantly more wood in our forests each year than we cut, and the local forestry literature has for seventy years amounted to one long lament about the lack of markets for small, non-timber quality wood that needs to be thinned out of the forest in timber stand improvement cuts. We could demand several hundred thousand more cords of wood annually and still be fine if we had a system for assuring good forestry practice was employed in the harvesting."[9]

By one estimate a house that normally uses 500 gallons of Number 2 fuel oil in a year could produce the same heat using a wood furnace with 3.6 cords of wood. (A cord of wood is a wood pile 4 feet wide, 4 feet high, and 8 feet long—or 128 cubic feet.) A house that uses 60,000 cubic feet of natural gas per year would require 3.1 cords of wood to produce the same heat using an airtight woodstove.[10] This is much better than the twenty to thirty cords of wood per house used in fireplaces each season in Colonial New England.[11]

Scrap wood, paper, and wood pellets

It's not necessary to burn logs. My husband and I augment our heat supply with scrap wood from our town dump. (If you haven't done so already, seek out the trash-handling center closest to your home. If nothing else, it will provide a modern-day archaeological study of today's wasteful era. My casual estimate is that about half of what people throw away could still be used.) Small pieces of two-by-fours and untreated wood trim show up there every week. Because our woodstove is a secondary heat source, we have tried to make the wood supply as cheap as possible. Occasionally I've bartered with a friend for a trunk full of split logs. He gives me the logs from his hand-cut supply (from his own land), and I give him a loaf or two of bread for his family. Not everyone has such easy-to-please friends who love chopping extra wood. Nevertheless, scrap wood is abundant. I see enterprising men in pickup trucks collecting the utility company's leavings from tree-trimming jobs. Construction debris may await you at the local lumberyard or renovating business.

Warning! When using scrap wood, be absolutely sure that it wasn't pressure treated. Identify pressure-treated wood—which is usually milled and cut for decks, lawn furniture, fences, docks, and other outdoor structures—by its greenish cast and smooth finish. It also has a distinct smell. Research studies have concluded that the common chemical used before 2004 to preserve such wood—chromated copper arsenate (CCA)—seeps out of the wood into soil. When it burns, both the smoke and ashes contain hazardous chemicals that could be absorbed through the skin or leach through soil to contaminate groundwater.[12] Other ways to burn natural products safely are to buy pellet stoves that burn wood pellets, corn, or paper pellets. Experts recommend that you don't burn these in regular woodstoves but in stoves designed for these fuels. Pellets are easy to load and very dry—about 3 percent to 4 percent moisture—so they burn more efficiently than wood. Pound for pound, these cost roughly the same as wood. You can buy pellets through a woodstove dealer or home store.[13]

Burning wood efficiently

Wood must be dry enough to burn efficiently. If you buy wood from a firewood cutter, you can be fairly sure the supply has been seasoned, which means it sat drying for one year. But if you scavenge wood, be sure that any green wood you collect sits for a season to dry out. Green wood doesn't look literally green, but some species do have a green tinge in the pulp. When you split a green log, the inside is supple. Green wood contains 40 to 70 percent moisture, says Ashford, Connecticut, wood expert John Bartok, a retired engineer from the University of Connecticut Cooperative Extension Center. Seasoned firewood is about 20 percent moisture. Burning green wood won't produce as much heat as burning seasoned wood. Burning green wood greatly diminishes the stove's efficiency. The stove can't get as hot, and creosote can build up in the inside, creating a fire hazard in the chimney.[14]

Switching from Oil or Natural Gas to Wood in a 1,500-square-foot House

The following chart illustrates something of a hypothetical situation. It assumes that the woodstove is situated in a central location of a small house and provides all of the heat. The experts tell me this is very doable.

Most of us use woodstoves only occasionally to provide some of the heat for our homes. I use this example to show you the most you could get if you decided to burn wood and were devoted to that as your heating method.

In this example, I assume you are comparing the cost of a new woodstove to that of a furnace already in place. I assume that the cost of a cord of wood remains constant. Wood quality can affect how well it heats. Pine is less efficient than shagbark, which is the most efficient. I use white ash as an example because it's a middle-of-the-road wood that reflects a cord of mixed species.

When you consider costs, factor in chimney sweeping each year (about $75) and a maintenance cost of a few hundred dollars after the third year or so.

While all wood provides the same amount of energy per pound, the amount of wood per pound varies greatly from species to species. For instance, according to Iowa State University, a pound of basswood weighs twenty-five pounds per cubic foot, while shagbark hickory weighs fifty-one pounds per cubic foot.

	Stove model and cost	Wood needed/ season	Buying your wood	Cutting your own wood	Oil furnace	Natural gas	Notes
Stove model 1	Quadra-Fire 3100 Millenium, non-catalytic stove, about $1499	3.5 cords of decent hardwood	$200 a cord, total $650	Free	700 gallons at $4.42/ gallon, total $3,094	About $1,500 in 2008	If you have free wood, the stove pays for itself in the first season. If you buy the wood, the stove pays for itself in the second season.
Stove model 2	Quadra-Fire Santa Fe, wood pellet stove, about $2200	About 2 tons	About $600	Free	$3,094	$1,500	If you have free wood, the stove pays for itself in the first season. If you buy the wood, the stove pays for itself in the second season.

Sources: For stove models and prices, Gabe Stein of Preston Trading Post, Preston, CT. For cord wood prices, hearth.com. For oil and natural gas prices, Energy Information Administration of the U.S. Department of Energy. For maintenance estimates, Dirk Thomas, a chimney sweep from Vermont and the author of *The Wood Burner's Companion*.

The chart below, based upon data from the University of Missouri Extension, evaluates wood with a 20 percent moisture content. (It's crucial to aim for that percentage. Dry or season all cut wood for at least six months and preferably for a year to eighteen months.) Wood this dry provides about 7,000 Btu's of energy per pound.

Heating efficiency also depends on the stove's or furnace's efficiency and how well the house is insulated.

Comparing Firewood Efficiency

Wood	Million Btu's per cord	Gallons of fuel oil needed to equal one cord	Tons of coal needed to equal cord	Cubic feet, in hundreds, of natural gas needed to equal cord	Gallons of propane needed to equal cord	Kilowatt hours of electricity needed to equal cord
Osage orange	30.7	219.3	1.28	307	337.4	9,029
Shagbark hickory	29.1	207.9	1.21	291	319.8	8,559
Black locust	28.1	200.7	1.17	281	308.8	8,265
White oak	27	193	1.1	270	297	7,941
Red oak	25.3	181	1	253	278	7,441
Sugar maple	25	179	1	250	275	7,353
Ash	23.6	169	1	236	259	6,941
Black walnut	21.8	156	1	218	240	6,412

(continued on next page)

Comparing Firewood Efficiency, cont.

Wood	Million Btu's per cord	Gallons of fuel oil needed to equal one cord	Tons of coal needed to equal cord	Cubic feet, in hundreds, of natural gas needed to equal cord	Gallons of propane needed to equal cord	Kilowatt hours of electricity needed to equal cord
Hackberry	21.6	154	0.9	216	237	6,353
Red elm	21.4	153	0.9	214	235	6,294
Sycamore	20.7	148	0.9	207	227	6,088
Elm	20.1	144	0.8	201	221	5,912
Shortleaf pine	19	136	0.8	190	209	5,588
Red cedar	18.9	135	0.8	189	208	5,559
Box elder	17.5	125	0.7	175	192	5,147
Cottonwood	16.1	115	0.7	161	177	4,735
Basswood	14.7	105	0.6	147	161	4,324

Source for figures: Publication G5450, University of Missouri Extension. See http://muextension.missouri.edu.

CHAPTER SIX

Harnessing a Backyard Stream: Micro-Hydroelectric Systems

Making electricity with falling water is one of the most simple and fascinating concepts modern civilization has ever perfected. On a large scale this requires giant dams to control the flow. But in someone's backyard stream, the dam can be quite small and the turbine no larger than a car motor. Of course you also need a backup method of providing electricity if a drought temporarily dries up the stream. For those who live near power lines, using a micro-hydro system might amount to a hobby, but perhaps not as expensive as building cars or flying around the world. The hardest part for anyone might be obtaining permits to install a micro-hydro system.

Using water for power is part of our ancient past. The first known dam was an earthen structure built in Egypt forty-five hundred years ago. (The rains washed it away the first year.) In order to achieve a good flow without limiting all power generation to waterfall-side sites, civilizations as far back as two thousand years ago wrestled the water into submission. Most of the time this meant damming a stream or river so that the water flow could be controlled—and creating a lake behind it. At first it involved placing wheels in the water flow; the turning wheels turned other machinery. By the mid-1700s, scientists worked on new machines that could convert water flow into direct current (DC). By the late 1800s the first hydroelectric power plant in the world went online in Wisconsin, producing alternating current (AC).[1]

Colonial Americans built small-scale hydroelectric systems that powered mills and machinery. Hydroelectric power isn't benign; it interrupts rivers, changes fish migration, and even alters the rotation of Earth ever so slightly, because the artificial lakes weigh so much. But water replenishes itself and doesn't make air pollution. If hydroelectric plants include fish ladders, the damage to fish life isn't as great.

Big dams continue to control water for power plants in the West and Northeast. The Hoover Dam across the Colorado River near Las Vegas, the Grand Coulee Dam across the Columbia River in the state of Washington, and the Shasta Dam across the Sacramento River in California all divert rivers into energy production for millions of customers. These dams are huge. Cars can drive across the top of the Hoover Dam, through which water travels at least 420 feet, powering seventeen turbines and providing 2,080 megawatts of power. The Grand Coulee Dam, the largest concrete structure in the world, holds back Columbia River water to make Lake Roosevelt, which reaches from the dam to the Canadian border, 150 miles long. The Shasta Dam's spillway is 438 feet long, creating the tallest human-made waterfall in the world.[2]

In the 1990s smaller dams—many left over from abandoned mills—began to be dismantled, along with warnings that dams threatened fish or waterways. We had barely gotten used to the modern ethic, most notable in the 1990s, of breaching or removing small dams on many of the lesser rivers across the United States, when the micro-hydroelectric movement started to regather steam. And so it's natural to wonder whether such systems hurt the wildlife that live in the flow of streams or change the vegetation in them. Large reservoirs hold a lot of dead plants that encourage the growth of the kinds of bacteria that absorb mercury, which might be in the soil, and that fish may eat. But in a micro-hydro system, the impounded water area is small.

One man's system

Richard G. Mackowiak lives in Eastford, Connecticut, on the tiny Still River, which joins the Natchaug River downstream. The hydroelectric plant in his yard dates to 1830. Mackowiak says that he set out to build, install, and maintain a new hydroelectric plant on his property that would power his entire house (including the heating system) and allow him to sell power back to the electric company. His intentions became a reality.

Mackowiak and his wife and son live comfortably on the power, and he sells extra to Connecticut Light & Power. "On the average I make almost twice as much as I need, so in addition to supplying all my electricity, they do send me a small check once a month," he says. "I think I got a check for $34 or something. It's the energy portion of the electric bill."

In Connecticut all the various surcharges bring the kilowatt-hour price to more than 18 cents an hour (of which perhaps 7 cents is the energy itself). Mackowiak must pay that price like any customer, and he can sell his power back only at the wholesale rate. The result pleases him, even if he isn't making a lot of money. "We don't have any energy costs of any kind," he says. "There are no oil deliveries here. There is no gas line coming in off the street."

Mackowiak owned a business that sold hydroelectric equipment and recently sold out to a partner after twenty years. In other words, he intimately understands his equipment and knows how to take care of it—as you will need to if you want to try this. "I've done everything by myself," he says. "I'm the only one who knows the equipment in and out. I built it by myself, and I'm the only one who takes care of it. That puts me in a predicament. When I go on vacation, there's no one here to watch it. It's not like the furnace that you have down in your basement; you have the guy come down once a year and see if it's still there. You need to know a little bit about everything to keep it running—mechanical, electrical, or carpentry repair."

Mackowiak does not believe he'll live long enough to recoup his investment. "Economically, I don't think anybody could justify it. But there are a lot of people like myself who do it because it's enjoyable."

The whole process took him so many years, and the cost is so tied up in his own time and labor, that he hasn't attempted to put a price on it. But he is glad he did it. "Whenever I tell the story as I'm telling it to you, I always have a smile on my face. . . . [It] has taken a long time, but I think that's part of what makes it rewarding. Even building this project here in the backyard. It took me twelve years working on weekends to put the thing back together. To see it actually finished and working, it was just great."

How to get started

Be certain your property contains the following features:

"Head" and "flow" in your waterway. The water in the stream or river must drop a distance before the water collects in a pipe to run a turbine. A waterfall is ideal, but most hydro systems, from the largest to the smallest, achieve *head* with an impoundment of water behind a dam. Systems can also work if established in the run of the river or stream, without an impoundment. The dam holds back water except a small amount that rushes through at high pressure. The stream or river must also contain enough water moving through at a fast enough rate. The amount of water in the stream, which hydro contractors always call *flow,* is measured in gallons per minute. The higher the flow, the more power you can harness.

A small residential hydroelectric system includes a box that collects the water, called the *diversion;* the pipeline to create pressure; the turbine and generator; and a route for the water to flow back into the stream or river, which is called the *tailrace.*

Ability to collect water at the highest point. The place where your micro-hydro system begins is at the highest point where you can set up the *intake.* Here is where the dam would hold back water and release it as pressurized head; or, perhaps, you have a waterfall and all you need is to place a screened pipe in it. It's important for the water to move quietly before it enters the intake pipe, since air or debris can damage the turbine below. The pipeline, or *penstock,* is the term for this quiet area of water.

Enough flow to provide 300 to 400 watts of continuous output. This will provide a household with all of the nonheating electricity it should need. (A basic rule of using alternative energy is to avoid using electricity to heat *anything.*)

In order to determine whether you can provide enough, your next step is to find a contractor. You need a turbine that is specially designed for your stream's or river's conditions. Some turbines work immersed in water, while others sit mostly above the surface, activated when the flow hits.

To generate a supply of AC, you will need more water than if you install a system that stores DC in batteries. (The battery

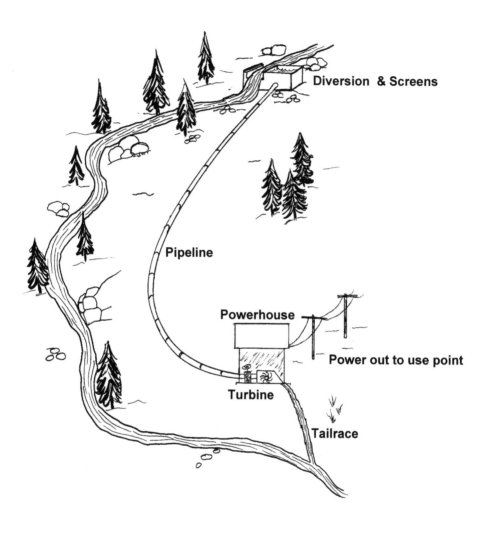

A small residential hydroelectric system includes a box that collects the water, called the diversion; the pipeline to create pressure; the turbine and generator; and a route for the water to flow back into the stream or river, which is called the tailrace. (Illustration by Dawn New, courtesy of Canyon Hydro of Deming, Washington)

system must connect to an inverter to convert the DC to AC.) A contractor can help decide what sort of system you can install. For resources see the Appendix.[3]

This small hydroelectric turbine converts moving water to electricity with a hidden belt on wheel, similar to the one propped on the outside. (Photo courtesy of Canyon Industries, Inc.)

Be realistic

Mackowiak makes it clear: A hydro system is expensive. Canadian micro-hydro dealer Paul Cunningham says that he actively discourages anyone who could otherwise hook into established electricity lines from trying hydro. But for those who live too far from electric lines to escape major costs of extending them to their property, an off-grid micro-hydro system could be cheaper than the cost of extending power lines.

Mackowiak says that you are best off using a dam that already crosses your stream. In New England that is not that difficult. "Usually they were all built with this in mind, to produce power," he says. "All I've done in the backyard is to repair something that someone built 150 years ago."

Structures in streams usually require permits from several agencies. Mackowiak's permits came through in three years. There were no migrating fish that required a fish ladder, but "there were many fish concerns. When the FERC [Federal Energy Regulatory Commission] studies my application for a license, they involve all the people." They include the state environmental department, the U.S. Army Corps of Engineers, the U.S. Fish & Wildlife Service, and other agencies—all of whom offer observations and suggestions for operating the equipment without hurting the wildlife.

As a result of his permit requirements, Mackowiak is not allowed to use all of the water in the river. In dry summers he has to turn off the turbine, sometimes for as long as two months. This ensures that enough water remains in the river for the fish.

All this means that you need some sort of a backup generator. In Mackowiak's case, he's hooked to the power grid, so whenever he isn't producing power, he's buying it. The flow of electricity to the house is never interrupted.

The realities of the grid

Hydro systems are specialized enough and expensive enough that most people who use them do not connect to the grid. "Ninety-nine percent of our customers are off-grid," says Cunningham, a partner in Energy Systems and Design of Sussex,

New Brunswick, Canada. He says that it's not even worth your while to try to compare the costs of staying connected to the power grid with getting your power from your stream or river. "If you try to make it look good, it won't," he says. It's too expensive. Also, you have to figure in that power from the grid is generally heavily subsidized. Figuring the environmental costs if we continue burning fossil fuels for most electricity is also quite complicated.

"The playing field is nowhere [near] level," Cunningham says. "Every day I have a conversation with somebody who thinks they are going to save money or make money. I say, you're not going to buy anything from me."

He's so tough with his words because he wants potential hydro owners to understand the commitment they'd make and the cost. He has little patience for the question of comparing utility-supplied electricity's cost to the cost of using a hydroelectric system. "Once people use the payback [question], I almost slam down the phone," he says.

Cunningham also says that if you do use an alternative technology like hydro, and if you do not connect to the grid, you will naturally use less power. "If you have utility power, you tend to overuse and use rivers of energy and think you're using a trickle," he says. "Almost invariably the people who call me up and want to do this, they don't want to use less power. They want to switch seamlessly from one type of power to another."

He says, "The point I will make again and again is: If you can reduce your needs . . . why would you invest in anything? First thing I said was: Over 99 percent of our customers are off-grid. That's our customer base. The people who are on-grid, as soon as I find out they have commercial power, I try to do away with them, in a gentle way."

CHAPTER SEVEN

Alternative Cars

Little looks good for the future of gasoline right now: not the price, not the projections of a long-term supply, not the automobile's major contribution to carbon dioxide in the atmosphere. The only positive thing we can say is that it still gets most people in the Western Hemisphere where they need to go. As petroleum begins its slow decline and countries look for ways to slow the human-caused effects of climate change, cars are losing their allure for many of us.

While we wait to see if fuel cells will be a major alternative, the only good option to save money and gasoline is to drive less. Unfortunately, this is a skill lost on many Americans, partly because we're lazy but also because highways run our lives—have you checked passenger-bus schedules recently? It also has to do with how our towns and suburbs have been constructed with a heavy reliance on roads and commercial areas removed from residential areas. I'm no poster child for low mileage, although I am trying to change. I drive a lot (I'm a devoted car recycler and don't own the most efficient model; right now I drive a 2000 Ford Taurus we bought at our local senior housing complex for $2,000). But all of us must face the fact that our driving habits and the efficiency of our cars need some upgrades. Cars and trucks burn 27 percent of all the energy consumed in the United States—up 2 percent from three decades ago. Cars and trucks account for 79 percent of carbon emissions.[1]

The good news is that the efficiency of American-made vehicles is finally showing signs of improvement after many years of energy gobbling. Congress has finally passed a law requiring higher mileage, but it won't take effect for a few years. The Energy Independence and Security Act of 2007 calls for the entire fleet of cars and light trucks to average thirty-five miles per gallon starting in 2011. As a whole, the fleet averages about twenty-seven miles per gallon as of 2008. In the last few years that average finally has surpassed the 1908 Model T Ford, which traveled twenty-five mpg. We also can be glad that finally people are turning away from the sport-utility vehicle, which is a light truck, and demanding something smaller for families.[2]

The whole thing is rather embarrassing. In Europe, cars average more than forty miles per gallon. If you've decided to get better gas mileage, the fight is a little easier than it was a few years ago, though. It's easier to buy an alternative vehicle today than it was only a few years ago, but the demand is greater than the supply. It's typical to have to get on a waiting list for a gas-electric hybrid car—perhaps as long as several months. Until the mid-2000s the automobile industry had delayed mass-producing alternative vehicles and even spent some effort arguing against their use. Lobbyists spent a few decades arguing that changing factories, plans, and equipment would be very bad for the embattled automotive industry. Only very recently has this litany softened and started to change in response to customers' demand.

Let's consider the short history of hybrids in the United States. The first hybrid vehicle wasn't available in the United States until 1999, when the Honda Insight first went on sale here. The next year, Toyota began selling its Prius in the United States. Since 1999, 660,000 hybrid cars have sold in the United States, and because they use so much less gasoline, they have saved 5.5 million barrels of oil total. (To gain some perspective, the United States imports about 12 million gallons per day.)[3]

In 2005 other alternative vehicles began to take off in numbers and popularity in the United States. Gas-electric hybrids have finally emerged in the ordinary American's consciousness. Hybrids use gasoline to power a battery system that allows the engine to switch periodically to straight battery power, saving a lot of fuel.

The number of gas-electric hybrids being produced is still small, but it is growing. Toyota was aiming to sell 175,000 Priuses in 2008, for example. There are now sixteen hybrids on the market. Toyota began producing its hybrid Camry model at its Georgetown, Kentucky, plant. Toyota said it would be able to produce 48,000 of the new hybrids each year in Kentucky.

It says something that Americans like the Toyota Prius, which today is the most popular hybrid car. More Americans

The best-selling hybrid, the Prius, is Toyota's third most popular car. (Photo courtesy of Toyota)

The Honda Fit is better than some of the hybrids, going 38 miles per gallon on the highway. (Photo courtesy of Honda)

bought this car in 2007 than the once very popular Ford Explorer SUV. That year, Prius sales increased by 69 percent over the previous year, to 181,221 cars.[4]

Other experiments went awry. When GMC recalled an electric pickup truck issued in limited quantities in California, electric-car lovers demonstrated. The zero emissions were nice, but the trucks did not save fuel because they relied on fossil fuel for the battery. Still, the public's anger over the demise of that first electric car showed how eager ordinary people were for something other than the typical gas-burning vehicle.

Hydrogen fuel cell cars

In May 2005 the House of Representatives passed the Clean Cars 2 initiative (HB 6908) to develop financial incentives for those who buy energy-efficient cars. In June the Connecticut State Assembly passed a bill to set up financial incentives for clean cars, the first such bill of its kind in the country.[5]

That same month, Honda lent its FCX (Fuel Cell Experimental), an experimental hydrogen fuel cell car, to journalist Jim Motavalli. He drove the car for 265 miles over a week, interrupted only by the car's trip in a trailer to a refueling station in upstate New York. Motavalli reported he was pleasantly surprised by the car's speed and efficiency—almost like a gas-powered car. The FCX can go only about 190 miles before refueling, and, so far, it's possible the car would last only about thirty thousand miles (not to mention that the country would need a network of hydrogen refueling stations). Why hydrogen cars have taken so long is a good question. At former president Jimmy Carter's inauguration in 1977, a hydrogen Cadillac was on display. Now, three decades later, the experts and the government predict that it would take another decade or two of research before the public could buy and use hydrogen cars.[6] (For more on how hydrogen fuel cells work, see chapter 4.)

How hybrid cars work

Hybrid cars run on both a gasoline engine and an electric motor. Brutally simplified, the gasoline engine runs the car and also charges the electric motor, which kicks in under certain conditions. When the driver stops the car to wait for someone in a driveway or at a stop sign, for example, the engine turns off completely, bringing on an eerie quiet. As the car-research Web publication Edmunds.com explains it, hybrids fall into two categories. Some hybrids run on only the electric motor at low speeds, and therefore get better mileage in city driving conditions; examples are the Toyota Prius and the Ford Escape Hybrid. But other hybrids are no better than a traditional car in city driving conditions, because the electric motor kicks in only to boost the gasoline engine when accelerating or going uphill. This second group of hybrids includes the Civic Hybrid.

The Edmunds.com Web editors explain, "a Toyota Prius accelerates from a standstill, the electric motor gets the vehicle rolling and continues to drive it up to around 25 mph before the gasoline engine automatically starts up. Under hard acceleration from a stop, the gas engine starts immediately to provide maximum power. . . . Because the electric motor is used so much at low speeds, the Prius and Escape get better mileage in the city than they do on the highway."[7]

But the Honda hybrid models use the electric motor only when the car needs a boost—"such as during hard acceleration from a stop, while climbing a hill, or passing other vehicles. As with normal, gas-powered cars, these hybrids get better fuel economy while cruising on the highway, as that is when the gas engine is least taxed."[8]

Although the electric motor runs off battery power, the hybrid technology automatically recharges itself through normal braking and coasting action. Here is how this works. The Ford Escape, Honda Civic, and Toyota Prius all use sealed nickel metal hydride batteries, or NiMH batteries, like the batteries that power cell phones and laptop computers. The number of individual battery cells varies from car to car. The Prius batteries rate nearly 274 volts; the Honda hybrids provide 144 volts; and the Ford Escape Hybrid rate 330 volts. As the car coasts on a downgrade, or when the driver puts the brakes on, the system reverses its polarity, and the electric motor automatically becomes a generator, converting the movement and braking into mechanical energy that the batteries store.[9]

A look under the hood of a Toyota Prius. Because most gasoline engines are more powerful than usually necessary, a hybrid-electric car has room for a small gasoline engine and an electric motor. The electric motor is powered by a battery that is fueled by the gasoline engine. Electronic controls make the car's various engines work together. (Photo courtesy of Toyota Motor Sales U.S.A.)

Public starting to scream for hybrids

The carmakers aren't producing as many hybrid cars as there are people who want them. They believe the general public isn't quite ready for this, but the group that is ready has grown fast. Toyota sold about 54,000 hybrid cars in 2004, according to Toyota Motor Sales spokesman Bill Kwong. Two years later that number had almost doubled, to 106,000. In 2007 Toyota increased its production and sold 180,221 by year's end. "In the beginning of 2007, Toyota said: You have been screaming for more, and here are 160,000, 170,000. It's incredible. People are just flocking to the showrooms to buy these things."[10]

Toyota's gas-powered cars still outstrip the Prius. The company manufactures more than six times as many gas-powered Corollas and Camrys, which are still at the number one spot.

"Prius is actually our third best-selling car," Kwong says. As of 2008 the great majority of Priuses were still manufactured in Japan, while the majority Camrys and Corollas are made in North America.[11] According to a Pew Research Center poll of about two thousand people in June 2008, most Americans are still more focused on finding more sources of oil to bring gas prices down than on conserving or regulating its use.[12]

What to Consider When Buying a Hybrid

It used to be a great truth of the auto industry that people who buy hybrid cars were die-hard conservationists, a decided minority. That's not true anymore. Drivers who wouldn't have touched a hybrid a few years ago have gotten on the waiting lists to buy them.

When you buy a hybrid, yes, you want to reduce the number one cause of global warming, auto exhaust. But this chart shows that hybrids can also be a money-saving choice. The higher gas prices climb, the better the deal.

My chart on page 101–102—while it uses an arbitrary set of conditions—clarifies that some hybrids pay for themselves quickly, while others do not. Most of the midsize hybrids pay for themselves if you tend to drive a car for several years before replacing it, or if the price of gasoline is high. For most larger hybrids the payback is only environmental—and extremely slight, at that.

The hybrid trucks barely save any gasoline. In order not to lose engine power, the engines use a milder hybrid, or "mybrid," technology that results in less efficiency than other hybrids offer. (You have to ask yourself if it's worth it at all to buy a hybrid truck. Wouldn't it be better to cut out one trip a week?)

I have compared major hybrid models on sale in late 2008 to similar nonhybrid cars, using hypothetical parameters. I did not take into account car repairs and maintenance. These are base models without extra features. I have averaged city and highway miles-per-gallon estimates from a number of sources.[13] My mileage figure assumes you'd drive about equal amounts on the highway and in town.

For comparison I chose nonhybrid cars very similar to the hybrids in size, engine size, and convenience, but these are not identical. The Honda Insight has no nonhybrid counterpart, so I compared it to Honda's most efficient nonhybrid, the Civic.

I worked with base prices without added features. I picked a middle-of-the-road yearly mileage figure and a gasoline price projected for 2009 by the U.S. Energy Information Administration. If you don't drive much, it will take you longer to recoup any car investment. On the other hand, you are doing the right thing not to drive much.

Finally, I make no claims that this is scientific. Fluctuating gas prices, differing driving habits, and inflation will alter the results. If you'd like, get out a calculator and play around with your own figures.

The more you study hybrids, the more obvious it is that choosing one is part of a comparison game. Some of them simply don't save a great deal of gas. Until the world switches over to a technology that doesn't burn petroleum, the only way to reduce emissions is to save gas. Consider this obvious point: You don't have to buy a hybrid to save gas. It's better to drive a car like the Toyota Yaris (thirty-four miles per gallon in the city, forty on the highway) or the Honda Fit (thirty-three miles per gallon in the city, thirty-eight on the highway) than any hybrid that uses more gas. These two cars ranked fourth and fifth on the list of most-efficient cars in 2007, compiled by the online car magazine Edmunds.com. (The first three on that list were the Toyota Prius, the Honda Civic Hybrid, and the Toyota Camry

How Long It Takes to Make Back Your Hybrid Car Investment

Hybrid Model	Base price	City mpg	Highway mpg	Average mpg	Yearly gas bill if driving 30,000 miles and if gas costs $4.10/gallon	Comparable nonhybrid car, price, average mpg, and yearly gas bill	Approximate length of time to recoup the extra cost of the hybrid, if gas costs $4.10/gallon
Ford Escape Hybrid	$26,640	34	30	32	$3,844	Ford Escape: $19,140; 25 avg. mpg; $4,920 gas bill	7 years (pay $7,500 more; save $1,076/yr)
Toyota Prius	$21,500	48	45	47	$2,645	Toyota Camry manual transmission: $18,920; 26 avg. mpg; $4,731 gas bill	1 year, 3 mos. (Pay $2,580 more; save $2,086/yr)
Toyota Camry Hybrid	$25,650	33	34	34	$3,672	Toyota Camry manual transmission: $18,920; 26 avg. mpg; $4,731 gas bill	6 years, 4 mos. (pay $6,730 more; save $1,059/yr)
Toyota High-lander Hybrid	$34,200	27	25	26	$4,730	Toyota Highlander: $27,500; 21 avg. mpg; $5,857 gas bill	Almost 6 years (pay $6,700 more; save $1,127/yr)

(continued on next page)

How Long It Takes to Make Back Your Hybrid Car Investment, cont.

Honda Civic Hybrid	$22,600	40	45	43	$2,860	Honda Civic Sedan manual transmission: $15,010; 30 avg. mpg; $4,100 gas bill	6 years (pay $7,590 more; save $1,240/yr)
Lexus GS Hybrid	$55,800	22	25	24	$5,234	Lexus GS 350: $44,550; 23 avg. mpg; $5,348 gas bill	99 years (pay $11,250 more; save $114/yr)
Saturn Aura Green Line	$24,550	24	32	28	$4,393	Saturn Aura $21,055; 26 avg. mpg; $4,731 gas bill	10 years, 4 mos. (pay $3,495 more; save $338/yr)
Lexus RX Hybrid	$42,980	26	24	25	$4,920	Lexus RX: $39,100; 20 avg. mpg; $6,308 gas bill	Under 3 years (pay $3,880 more; save $1,388/yr)
Nissan Altima Hybrid	$24,480	35	33	34	$3,616	Nissan Altima 2.5 S manual transmission: $20,470; 28 avg. mpg; $4,473 gas bill	4 years, 6 mos (pay $4,010 more; save $857/yr)
Chevy Malibu Hybrid	$24,545	24	32	38	$4,393	Chevy Malibu LS: $20,550; 26 avg. mpg; $4,731 gas bill	Under 12 years (pay $3,995 more; save $338/yr)

Sources: For prices and mileage estimates, individual car manufacturers. For technology notes, *Wired* magazine (April 2005); www.fueleconomy.gov.

Hybrid.) A regular Toyota Corolla was the sixth most-efficient car on that list. Heck, even a Hyundai Accent (it came in eighth) saves more gas than most of the hybrids manufactured now. It gets thirty-five miles per gallon on the highway.

This leads to another obvious point, but one I still struggle to remember: If we don't drive at all, we don't use gas at all. In other words, we should still think about walking, biking, and taking the train or bus whenever and wherever possible.

Source: Gas mileage and efficiency rankings for regular and hybrid cars are from www. edmunds.com.

CHAPTER EIGHT

Conservation: Not a New Idea

The most obvious tactic to reduce energy usage—using less— tends to catch on in the United States when a crisis hits. And these times just might qualify. Oil prices are surging. Americans are starting to think before they drive. Oil companies are extracting new sources in areas previously thought a waste of time, like "tight gas" reserves in Colorado. The middle and lower classes struggle to pay basic bills. House foreclosures are common news. And yet there's still an air of denial. I think that we Americans still think unlimited electricity and heat and technology are basic rights. It's so difficult to undo the assumptions born of a half-century of inexpensive energy.

Have you ever noticed that when policy makers and energy companies predict future electricity supplies, for example, they talk about meeting customers' *demand?* They might recommend that people conserve energy, but mainly they consider the challenges of meeting whatever *demand* the people present. For instance, in its 2007 annual report ExxonMobil predicted the world would continue to be hungrier and hungrier for energy through 2030 as the rising population "continues to advance and seek better living standards." As the gross domestic product increases by about 3 percent a year, the company announced, so too will the energy demand, by about 1.3 percent per year.[1]

What are we demanding? An excessively comfy life? Whatever people happened to use last year and the year before, increased to match the rising population? Demand encompasses their best guess at all of the electricity people need and want. It covers necessities like heat, cooking, industry, and essential trips and nonessentials like appliances, air conditioners, second and third televisions, big cars, lights left on in empty houses, and wasteful uses of everything. When utilities brace for brownouts in the summer and discuss meeting demand, perhaps they are merely trying to make money. Some of our power uses are necessary, and some of them aren't. Our failure to distinguish between needs and wants does not put all of our power demands in the same category as a hospital's needs. In the residential sector, "demand" is a label that shields us from the heroic efforts our energy systems make to generate power on our behalf.[2]

There is one state where that is not true: California. There, the push to cut energy use goes back to the 1970s and the promotion of alternatives in this millennium has been called "the new gold rush."[3] Governor Arnold Schwarzenegger initiated a "million solar roofs" campaign to encourage homeowners to install solar photovoltaics, and like many states and regions, it has started a cap-and-trade program for industries to reduce greenhouse gas emissions. Industries are granted a certain number of pollution credits based on their emissions; heavier polluters buy credits from cleaner companies, and the number of credits granted goes down over a period of years as the standards for cleaner emissions stacks go up.[4]

But most important for this discussion is how individual Californians act. Californians, per capita, use less electricity than the rest of the country. Since the mid-1970s, even as its population has increased, California has kept its electricity use at the same level while the rest of the country's per capita use has increased by about 50 percent. One example of how the state responds to the threat of losing power came in 2001, when

Californians achieved the great feat of reducing their electricity usage by 11 percent in one month compared to the same month in the previous year.

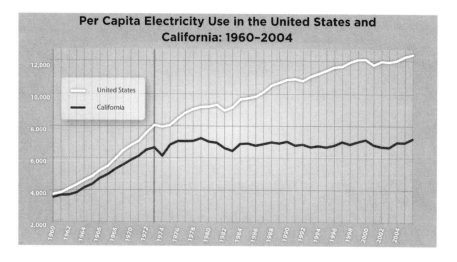

Per Capita Electricity Use in the United States and California: 1960–2004

Californians' electricity use, per capita, has remained basically the same for three decades, while the nation's has risen steadily. (California Energy Commission)

In the rest of the country, the exception to our dismal record of using power is in energy intensity—the amount of energy required to produce $1 worth of power. Thanks to innovations in equipment, appliances, and systems, energy intensity is falling by about 2 percent per year in the United States (and about 1.5 percent worldwide). In recent years China's energy intensity has risen, though, and certainly that is because Americans are relying more on Chinese factories.[5]

When it comes to energy consumption, a crisis can lead to savings. When electricity costs more, Americans use less, and that's happening now.[6]

Supply powerfully nudges us. From time to time, those government leaders who are worried about energy supplies (like Schwarzenegger) carry the flag for conservation, often with impressive results. We have seen that in California. But rarely do calls to conserve move Americans. People still discuss the ineffectiveness of former President Jimmy Carter dressed in a blue sweater as he urged Americans to use less energy. In 2001 President George W. Bush's press secretary, Ari Fleischer, said that reducing energy consumption was "a big no. . . . The president believes that it's [consuming energy] an American way of life." So in 2005, after Hurricane Katrina and Hurricane Rita, when Bush urged Americans to drive their cars less as oil supplies were uncertain, the country didn't take it seriously. Bush himself connected the need to conserve to the disruption in oil supplies. He told the public that if they could eliminate unnecessary car trips, "that would be helpful."[7]

Contrast this to the rally-the-troops approach in Japan. In spring 2005, Japan's government began a unique publicity campaign to inspire its citizens to use less electricity. It asked Japanese white-collar workers to stop wearing suits in the summer so that the air-conditioning could be set to a warmer temperature. To push the new dress code, Japan's environment ministry promoted a casual uniform it called "Cool Biz." The look included cotton shirts and conservative pants, but no jackets. "The government will take the lead in prevention of global warming," Prime Minister Junichiro Koizumi was quoted as saying in the *New York Times*. "From this summer, government is planning to start no necktie, no jacket." (Japanese men shunned an earlier casual business campaign in the 1970s, when the government pushed a suit with cut-off sleeves.)[8]

Perhaps conservation is so difficult in everyday American life because we don't see ourselves as we truly are. We don't see how our decisions about where and how to live use up energy. Consider the exurban development explosion in places like Colorado, where houses are going up on large lots scattered across a wide expanse of previously open countryside. Each year over the last four decades 144,000 acres of Colorado farmland have disappeared under other kinds of uses.[9]

Similar statistics greet you in most other regions of the United States, too. The energy toll this kind of development takes on our resources became clear in the 2000 U.S. Census. The average commute to work from the exurbs, the outer ring about fifty miles from Denver, was thirty-eight minutes, the Census reported, compared to twenty-four to twenty-six minutes from closer-in suburbs and Denver. "A commuter who drives 50 miles to work—25,000 miles a year—pumps out enough carbon dioxide, a key greenhouse gas, to fill a Goodyear blimp."[10]

In many towns in northeastern Connecticut, the last largely rural region from Washington to Boston, housing developments are cropping up at a fast rate. The increases in long-distance commuting between 1990 and 2000 in northeastern Connecticut were higher than the national average. The intrepid workers were commuting by car to as far away as Boston and New York.[11]

We're losing our untrammeled land at great cost to the environment. Not only are animal habitats being reduced, we're using more energy to live, scattered on large plots of land across the regions. The people who buy houses in the former backcountry love nature, I'm betting, which is why they want to live out in it. Many of the homeowners I have read about in the last few years are young to middle-aged professional adults who telecommute part of the week and relish their part-time semirural lives, away from the hubbub. They spend hours and lots of gas getting to and from their refuges. But now they are starting to realize that they aren't the only people doing this, discovering they are not intrepid individualists but part of a trend. It is easier to waste energy and resources in this way of life—especially if these people treat their outposts as if they were suburbs by making frequent trips into town.

If they are true to their ideals, assuming they moved to the exurbs because they value the land, they'd avoid daily car trips to the places from which they fled. Or they'd find another method of travel. But they can't; not today. The trolley lines of the early twentieth century no longer exist. Trains are rare, too. So there is a responsibility that goes along with the decision to move far away from services, and the responsibility includes the need to save energy—to live more truly like a hermit, not just to do so for a few hours at a time.

Saving energy happens not only on the road but also in how you live. It happens within the walls of your house or apartment. In the last few decades, manufacturers have designed energy-efficient appliances that save a great deal of power over the appliances they replaced. The most dramatic improvements are in the new refrigerators and washing machines, two of the largest energy eaters at home. Improved house-building techniques trap heat indoors in the winter and cool air in the summer.

In other ways we've made little progress in conserving energy. During the energy crisis of the mid-1970s, two engineers suggested that the best ways to cut home energy use would be, first, to insulate houses; second, to buy more efficient air conditioners; and third, to take buses or trains. Looking at these three recommendations in 2008, it seems they remain good suggestions. That is, we still need to follow them.

First, consider the advice to insulate houses. The U.S. Department of Energy reports that homeowners pay for, and send outside, as much energy through badly insulated doors and windows as the Alaskan pipeline can deliver each year.[12]

Next, consider air conditioners. We should still try to reduce the power they use, but doing this is challenging because air-conditioning has taken over the indoor world since the 1970s. Efficient air conditioners alone can't reduce power when the number of buildings that use air-conditioning outweighs those that do not.

The energy crisis engineers' third idea, to take the bus or train, has remained only a hope in those places that weren't already relying on public transportation. The car still rules suburban, exurban, and rural America. Public transportation is limited to the very large cities. It was the best in the world in 1900, when trolley lines extended for great distances into backwater places. In 1923 the number of streetcar riders in the United States was 15.7 billion. By 1929 it had dropped to 14.4 billion, and by 1940 to 8.3 billion. Cars and buses took the place of the torn-out trolley lines. The passenger railroads crashed somewhat later, in the 1950s, when the government subsidies went to the air and automobile routes, bankrupting the railroads over the next twenty-five years or so.

"Unlike European governments, Washington treated public transportation as if it were a private business, while regarding the motorcar as worthy of immense public subsidies," wrote Kenneth T. Jackson, Columbia University historian and author. "Indeed, Senator Gaylord Nelson of Wisconsin reported that between 1945 and 1980, 75 percent of government expenditures on transport went for highways, and only 1 percent went to public buses, trolleys, or subways. The inevitable result of the bias in American policy, a bias that began even before the

Interstate Highway Act of 1956 and one that has no counterpart in either Europe or Asia, was that by 1991 the United States had the world's best road system and very nearly its worst public transit offerings."[13]

In order to follow the advice to use the car less, we'd have to change our lives. But we can't leave the car at home if we live in one of the many, many places where it's our only means (aside from walking or bicycling, that is) to get to work or school. If work or school is more than a mile or two from home, that demands a sort of sacrifice that people shouldn't have to make. But we can begin to examine the number of unnecessary trips we make in our cars. In the days of more common public transportation and fewer cars per household, people didn't make a few trips of ten, twenty, or fifty miles in a day —just to find a good sale or visit a new store. They did errands closer to home. Today in most places it's just so easy to jump in the car. Our way of life, our expectations of endless energy, still drives our deepest behavior.

Since the late 1990s, a number of groups have sprung up to encourage people to walk in cities and towns where cars have taken on the job of feet on the sidewalks. These groups differ from the exercise walking movement (touted on most supermarket-check-out magazine racks as ways to walk off the fat around your middle). Walking has even begun to attract serious research attention. It's a reasonable way to travel that costs nothing and gives people exercise. Every October an American group organizes "Walk-to-School Day." The group America Walks encourages people to rethink their routines and to take back the streets.[14]

At the same time, we have started going farther to do things that enhance our lives, and if we have to give these up, our lives would go backward. My high school age daughter, for instance, goes to school, visits friends, volunteers, and takes lessons in far-flung towns, requiring drives of twenty to forty miles round-trip. She now drives herself, although she once took a bus. Thirty years ago her routine might have been different. As soon as gas prices rose, she began to share rides with her friends, and I expect that to continue. Our older daughter is in college in a small city. She walks and takes the train for most of her mobility. She is learning, and we're being reminded, how it's possible in many areas to live without a car.

Expecting endless energy supplies might be a modern trait, but it comes from the incredible plenty around us. When problems pinch the energy supplies, we still have the ability to conserve energy, because humans have always done that. People of long ago conserved energy for fear the supply would run out, while they conducted their lives only to provide what was enough—and no more. But in today's world of science and exploration, where growth is considered good, this attitude doesn't prevail. Former environmental policy maker Lindsey Grant points out that going back to before 1300, people did not believe that economic growth was a natural force. "Then came the Renaissance, which led to the Age of Exploration to the new world and new wealth," he wrote. "It started the agricultural and industrial revolutions and set in motion a worldwide scientific enterprise that is still accelerating. . . . That period has lasted, with minor interruptions, for six centuries. . . . It is a formidable belief system, but its proponents have forgotten that its origins were not in population growth, but in the Black Death, the most widespread and severe population collapse in human history." It left survivors with more farmland and more wealth.[15]

The term *energy conservation* dates only to the environmental movement of the 1970s. In earlier industrial times, it was called *energy efficiency,* and it referred only to how well appliances, industrial components, and systems operated. Of course people used less energy if the supply was dwindling. On the frontier of America, pioneers conserved coal because it was so expensive to ship. In the 1970s Americans conserved energy only because of the Arab oil embargo. For those who grew up in that time, energy conservation presented itself as something we would not have to practice forever. It was supply based. The sooner environmentalists today accept this connection, the better the chance that we can make conservation part of the nation's energy policy, which so far it is not.

It would be nice to believe that the environmental movement that took off in about 1969 and lasted through the late 1970s was the result of our realization that we were hurting the planet. Some of it was just economics, though. In 1975 the Congressional Research Service compiled a series of documents about energy conservation. The readings included presentations before Congress on conservation; articles from David B. Large's book *Hidden Waste: Potential for Energy Conservation,* which the Conservation Foundation published in 1973; journal articles on power generation; energy use on farms; and reports on energy policy proposals.

In the introduction to the collection, an unnamed author writing for the collection's producer, the U.S. Senate's Committee on Interior and Insular Affairs, wrote: "In the past it was less costly to waste fuel than to use it efficiently. However, now, as a result of higher fuel costs, fuel scarcity, and our national dependency on foreign sources, energy conservation has been recognized as a national imperative." Up to that time energy policies were built on encouraging "industry to meet whatever demand is created in the marketplace." And that would have to change. (These words sound as if someone could have said them around the time oil prices began to shoot up in 2004.)

One of the articles reprinted in the congressional collection first appeared in the journal *Science* in 1974. Hans H. Landsberg wrote that the oil and natural gas shortages had changed the way people were thinking. "The United States has entered an era of profound alteration in traditional patterns and trends in the field of energy," he wrote. "Although the Arab oil embargo of recent months has greatly aggravated the crisis, the underlying causes lie farther back in the past and hopes of long-term remedies lie well into the future." He said the trouble had begun a few years before, when natural gas suppliers stopped hooking up new customers, heating oil shortages closed some schools and public buildings, midwestern farmers worried about getting enough fuel, and gas stations began shortening hours. Abroad, the Organization of Petroleum Exporting Countries (OPEC) revised contracts to deny access to supplies and "drastic, unilateral price boosts, with grave economic and political ramifications."[16]

Clearly the mood in the mid-1970s was one of crisis, and I sense between the lines of the congressional energy readings that the country was up to gathering its courage to get through it. Gary Althen says in his book *American Ways,* "Americans cling to these values: individualism, equality, informality, progress, speed, and assertiveness. Not on the list are frugality and conservation. Still, it's the American way to cope through hard times, and that mentality could change how we use electricity, gasoline, and other energies."[17]

You might think that today you are ready to step outside the American mainstream. You want to save energy because waste makes no sense, ethically. And I agree with you. But this kind of altruism has little track record in modern America, and everywhere you look, you find a sober truth emerging. Conservation is barely a micro-trend. Humans, particularly modern American humans, don't seem inclined to link every small act of comfort at home to the burning of fuel or every small act of sacrifice to the greater good of the community. There seems to be one reliable way human beings in any country can be made to conserve energy, and that is if the supply is limited or cut off. Here are the ways this could play out:

- We would have to use less energy because it would be against the law to use above a certain amount. This seems unlikely just on the merit of a law, unless something actually happened to the fuel supplies. The next scenario is more likely.

- We would have to conserve because energy supplies from distant sources are wobbly. We would start producing our own power, at home. Therefore, we wouldn't want to work harder than necessary to provide for ourselves, so we would naturally conserve energy, out of that innate trait of self-interest.

Paul Cunningham, who produces micro-hydroelectric systems in Canada for people who live away from power lines, believes most people don't realize how little power they actually need to live. "If you were using the minimal amount of power—lights, refrigeration, washing machine—that only takes about $20 a month worth of power."[18] The rest, he says, goes into waste or into the various appliances that heat things (like hot-water heaters, dryers, and irons). Anything that heats uses a tremendous amount of power.

"If there are 720 hours in a typical month, we get 216 kilowatt-hours per month. If you are paying 10 cents a kilowatt-hour, that's $21.60. If you're using more than that, then you have room to improve,"[19] says Cunningham.

Cunningham adds that to run a household with four people using standard appliances, as he's outlined above, requires 300 watts of continuous power. Asked if we Americans are living like spoiled brats using too much energy because subsidies make it cheap, he says yes.

He makes the sensible case that if you choose to live off the power grid, you will necessarily waste less. "If you have unlimited power, you probably will leave the lights on, and you will buy things that use more power," he says.[20]

Looking back on the occasional emergencies or experiments when people managed to change their ways clarifies how easy it is to cut back on energy use. With ordinary restraint the American public can redefine what the utilities and government love to call our energy "demand."

Consider the California rolling blackouts of 2001. The state predicted rolling blackouts due to a lack of electricity for the expected demand, so a huge campaign unfolded to get the state through the summer. Organizations handed out compact fluorescent bulbs, and the power use did go down. Comparing two almost identical days in 2000 and 2001, weather wise, the statewide power use was 44,906 megawatts on August 2, 2000, versus 40,384 megawatts on August 17, 2001. Seventy-nine percent of a surveyed group reported that they had cut their energy use in some way.

Then consider this bizarre experiment in saving hot water in a college athletic field house in 1982 and 1983. Researchers set out to test the power of suggestion on the length of hot showers in the locker room. First they posted signs in the bathrooms that said, SHORT SHOWERS SAVE ENERGY. As a result, 6 percent of the students took shorter showers. When a larger sign replaced the first, 19 percent cut back their showers, but people complained about the annoying reminder sign. When the researchers planted a student volunteer in the showers—with the instructions to turn off the water while soaping up whenever someone else was showering in an adjacent stall—49 percent of students did the same. The percentage increased to 67 percent when two volunteers, instead of one, enacted the water-saving measures.[21]

The college bathroom study proved that nudging people's consciences, even with a slightly annoying sign, can make people more responsible. It also proved that good behavior rubs off on others, leading to a higher level of responsible behavior. With that in mind, try the conservation tips listed in the next chapter—assuming you don't perceive the list as an annoying written reminder—and then watch while other people you know follow your example.

Most important, learn to think of the need to save energy as our response to a crisis that much of our world hasn't yet accepted. What many of the experts have been trying to tell us these last few years is that our definition of normal is going to change, even if there's no sign of it yet. Chauncey Starr, a physicist who pioneered study in nuclear reactors and president emeritus of the Electric Power Research Institute, said it well in 1973, and his words still speak to the way we "demand" energy: "The 'crisis' designation tends to be misleading," he wrote, "because it implies that quick-fix emergency steps should be taken to cure situations which have developed over many years. In fact, there are no quick fixes. Further, the practical realities of the situation have not yet required an immediate national 'crisis' response by applying true emergency measures—such as energy rationing and cessation of energy-consuming activities."[22]

CHAPTER NINE

Conservation Tips

Everything on the list here is straightforward, effective, and, as far as I know, legal. Why would I even have to note this? What irks me about the live-green lists you can now find in most periodicals are their cheery consumerist aspects and failure to mention, for example, that hanging laundry is currently not allowed in most private subdivisions in America, or that a motor scooter might save gas but it won't replace the car, so you have to consider its purchase as an extra. The live-green lists often suggest building new green houses, buying new green products, and moving to completely new green towns built somewhere on a piedmont. Everything you buy new to save energy you should weigh against the cost of the energy and materials to produce that thing. That's what we did when my family finally replaced our thirteen-year-old refrigerator that rattled and used ten times the energy of the new one.

Basic restraint is the ordinary person's best strategy to cut energy use. These suggestions assume that you are working with the dwelling you live in now and don't have unlimited funds or, if you are a renter, the power to make drastic changes in all of its systems. Most of these suggestions are to change behavior, switch or unplug appliances, treating power as a precious resource to be rationed with gratitude. These tips follow in no special order.

Turn off idle computers

In general the less time a computer is on, the longer it will last, and the more energy you save.

A computer uses the same amount of energy to turn on as it does to operate for about two seconds. It does not hurt a computer to turn it off ten or more times a day. The computer will wear out or become outdated before any wear and tear from that would affect it.

Plug the computer into a power strip, and whenever you are not using the computer for extended periods, turn it off using the switch on the power strip. If you use the buttons on the computer and leave it plugged in, it will continue to draw some power. If you have no power strip, unplug the computer when you aren't using it.

If you are not going to be on the computer for more than about twenty minutes, turn off the monitor. If the break is two hours or more, turn off the central processing unit (CPU) and the monitor. If you tend to go away and come back to the computer frequently during the day, turn off the monitor when you leave the desk. But if you aren't using it for four hours or more—and this counts for going to bed at night—turn off everything.

The only time you would leave the computer on is if you have a very old computer, say, fifteen years old, if the computer operates a phone, facsimile, printer, or security system, or if the computer is part of a network. On many computers, the "sleep" mode uses only a few watts, or practically nothing compared to the 200-plus watts or so of a typical desktop computer while running. So the sleep mode is close to the benefit of turning it off.

Source: U.S. Department of Energy, Energy Efficiency and Renewable Energy Web site, www .eere.energy.gov/consumer.

Heat and cool less

Recognize that heating and cooling systems use the most power in the house—up to half the total amount.

To get used to using less energy for heat, turn the thermostat lower in tiny increments over a period of a few weeks. The U.S. government's energy efficiency experts recommend keeping the thermostat at 68 degrees while you are awake and at between 53 and 58 degrees while you are sleeping (underneath multiple blankets). It is a misconception that thermostats use more energy reheating to the daytime temperature than they save by remaining low at night. When going away on vacation in all but the coldest months, turn heating or cooling systems completely off. To do this requires going to the unit and following instructions from the manual. Even in the summer, many furnaces remain turned on.

Sources: *Slash Your Energy Bills* by Allen Lawrence. San Antonio, Texas: Ambient Environmental Concerns, 1977. U.S. Department of Energy, Energy Efficiency and Renewable Energy program, www.eere.energy.gov/consumer.

Evaluate appliances—Upgrade to conserve

To figure watts when the appliance lists amps, multiply the number of amps by the number of volts provided through your wiring (usually 110 volts). Amps times voltage equals watts.

The electric stove: In his book *The Natural House*, Daniel D. Chiras advises people who are building new houses to install propane stoves. "The large burners on an electric stove use about 1,200 watts of power when on high. The smaller burners consume about 600 watts of power." Propane may not be ideal—because it's fossil fuel—but it's much cheaper than electric to use and the emissions are minimal.

The microwave oven: Energy experts will tell you that a microwave uses about half of the energy of a conventional oven—but beware. This is true only as long as you are not using the microwave in a wasteful way. *The Consumer Guide to Home Energy Savings* estimates that a microwave can bake a casserole more efficiently than any other oven (see the chart on page 121–122). But on the downside, people use microwaves for tasks better done on the stove, such as boiling a cup of water for tea, or using no heat at all, such as defrosting frozen food, which can be done in the refrigerator with a little forethought.

Source: Alex Wilson, Jennifer Thorne, and John Merrill, *The Consumer Guide to Home Energy Savings,* Washington, DC: American Council for an Energy Efficient Economy, 2003.

The following table is based on one in *The Consumer Guide to Home Energy Savings* comparing the cost of cooking a casserole in several ways. It assumes the cost of gas is 60 cents a therm (a therm is equal to one hundred thousand British thermal units, or Btu's), and electricity is 10 cents a kilowatt-hour.

Cost of Cooking

Appliance	Temperature (°F)	Time	Energy	Cost
Electric Oven	350	1 hour	2.0 kWh	$0.20
Electric Convection Oven	325	45 minutes	1.39 kWh	$0.14

(continued on next page)

Cost of Cooking, cont.

Appliance	Temperature (°F)	Time	Energy	Cost
Gas Oven	350	1 hour	0.112 therm	$0.09
Electric Frying Pan	420	1 hour	0.9 kWh	$0.09
Toaster Oven	425	50 minutes	0.95 kWh	$0.10
Electric Crockpot	200	7 hours	0.7 kWh	$0.07
Microwave Oven	"High"	15 minutes	0.36 kWh	$0.04

The refrigerator: Refrigerators use a good deal of a home's energy, and Americans seem to want more of them as time passes. The average size of American refrigerators increased by 10 percent from 1972 to 2001. And yet many refrigerators use much less energy today than they once did. The cost to run a typical new refrigerator (with automatic defrost and a freezer on top) is about $55 a year. In 1973 the typical refrigerator cost about $160 a year to run.

Sources: The Worldwatch Institute, www.worldwatch.org/pubs/goodstuff; Unitil (Fitchburg, Massachusetts), www.services.unitil.com; U.S. Energy Information Administration.

Refrigerators: Low-Energy Models

By law, all refrigerators carry a bright yellow tag labeled "EnergyGuide." It explains how much electricity in kilowatt-hours a refrigerator uses. Refrigerators the federal government certifies as low-energy always carry a tag labeled "Energy Star."

Here is a chart showing only a handful of the hundreds of models certified by the government as low-energy.

Refrigerator model	Kilowatt-hours per year (Energy Star estimate)
Abscold ARD1031F11RL Top freezer, 10.3 cubic feet	309
Amana ASD2524VEO Side-by-side 25.4 cubic feet	580
Crosley CRTE187J Top freezer, 18.3 cubic feet	383
Frigidaire 970-40982 Top freezer, 18.4 cubic feet	407
General Electric DTH18ZBX Top freezer, 18 cubic feet	387
Kenmore 253789780 Top freezer, 18.3 cubic feet	383
Maytag MFT2124EEO Top freezer, 21 cubic feet	416
Sun Frost RF-16 Top freezer, 14.3 cubic feet	254

Discard the old clothes washer

Dozens of clothes washers available today at reasonable prices save you from one-third to three times the energy older models use. The main feature to look for is a front-loading, tumble design that uses much less water (and therefore also less heat).

A front-loading washer uses much less water and energy than top-loaders, while a folding rack makes drying cost nothing, even on a rainy day. (Photo courtesy of author)

The following chart shows a fraction of the energy-saving clothes washers certified by the U.S. government through its Energy Star program. For more information see www.energystar.gov. The Web site includes a calculator tool to figure your savings. You can plug in details particular to your area, such as electricity rate and how many loads you do each year.

Energy-Saving Clothes Washers

Washer	Kilowatt-hours/year (Energy Star estimate)	Percent better (than the minimum federal standard)
Whirlpool LHWo-050	212	121%
Speed Queen CTSAO	184	96%
Miehle W1203	127	62%
Maytag Neptune MAH5500B	243	51%
Kenmore 4390	278	56%
GE WSXH208H	201	47%
Asko W6461	127	98%

Insulate the house

The single most important energy-saving project in a house is to insulate the attic. Next you want to insulate all the places where air leaks out. Insulating a typical house in the American West that uses natural gas heat can save an estimated 250 kilowatt-hours per year and, depending on many factors, between $750 and $3,500 per year over a thirty-year period.

"If you insulate first, and later on go out and buy a new heating system, the insulation means you can buy a smaller heating system," says Joel N. Gordes, an independent energy consultant from West Hartford, Connecticut. So it would be premature to invest in a geothermal heat pump or a new wood-stove and cord of wood if the heat you generate is going out of the cracks. Gordes says that adding up all the heat losses in a typical house amounts to a two-foot-square hole in the wall.

Insulation comes in several materials and thicknesses, each right for a specific area of a building and climate. The federal government has established a rating system for insulation, measuring its ability to resist the flow of heat (that is, its ability to hold heat inside). The higher the R-value, the thicker the insulation; but it's important not to use the wrong thickness. Insulation for the foundation and floors differs from that used on walls and ceilings. Insulation best in California wouldn't work in Tennessee.

It's not necessary to use commercial insulation, but you will have to do more work to learn how to use sheep's wool, straw, mixtures of straw and clay, cotton and plastic, and hemp—all of which can hold heat efficiently.

Foam gaskets and pads, new door sweeps, caulking, and even insulated board cut to fit windows will all help in older houses where air leaks through electrical outlets, under doors, around windows.

Make it a goal to replace the oldest of your windows. Put up storm windows earlier in the season than you have in the past, and leave them up longer into the spring. Change to thermal glass and use insulated curtains, available from most curtain catalogs.

Passive solar houses are sensible designs: They encourage the natural light to do much of the warming for you. But don't go building a whole new house just for this purpose (of course, if you're house hunting. . .). Work with the place you've got. If you live in a northern climate, plant deciduous trees near the house. In winter they'll let the sun through. In summer they'll cool the house. If you live in a desert climate, use awnings and blinds to block or let in the sun, depending on the season.

Sources: Fact sheets and publications by the Oak Ridge National Laboratory, www.ornl.gov (I recommend you peruse the whole Web site).Patty Limerick and Howard Geller, *What Every Westerner Should Know About Energy Efficiency and Conservation*, Boulder, CO: Center of the American West, University of Colorado, 2007, page 9; Daniel D. Chiras, *The Natural House: A Complete Guide to Healthy, Energy-Efficient, Environmental Homes*, White River Junction, Vermont: Chelsea Green Publishing Company, pp. 370–372; "A Consumer's Guide to Energy Efficiency," U.S. Department of Energy's Energy Efficiency and Renewable Energy program, www.eere.energy.gov/consumer.

Improve the furnace

It's difficult to avoid holding onto a furnace that burns oil, natural gas, or propane at least part of the year in most of North America. Even if you use a woodstove (see chapter 5), you might need a backup furnace that uses natural gas or Number 2 heating oil. The U.S. Environmental Protection Agency requires furnaces to divert a minimum of 78 percent of the fuel it burns to heating the house (the remainder goes up the chimney). Old furnaces can do much worse than this—about 65 percent—while the best of the new models are 97 percent efficient. You'll recoup your investment and help the environment. Maintain your furnace with annual cleanings to keep it running efficiently.

Source: Consumer Search, www.consumersearch.com.

Watch less television

A 36-inch television uses 133 watts of power. If it's turned on for 12 hours a day, 6 days a week for 313 days a year (allowing for when you're away from home), it will cost you $42.50 a year to run (at 8.5 cents a kilowatt-hour).

But if you leave the television on only six hours a day, the cost becomes $21.23 a year. Just two hours a day costs $7.07 a year. Okay, this doesn't sound like much, but the amount does add up with other conservation measures.

Source: Fact sheets on energy efficiency from U.S. Department of Energy, Energy Efficiency and Renewable Energy, www.eere.energy.gov/consumer.

Turn off lights and switch lightbulbs

At home improvement stores lately you might notice that compact fluorescent lightbulbs are front and center, stacked on the shelves of main aisles in a greater variety of shapes and wattages than ever before. Wal-Mart, the world's biggest retailer, has started promoting energy-efficient lightbulbs—labeled with the catchy Energy Star slogan "Change a Light. Change the World." It's part of the retailer's aggressive plan to sell more compact fluorescents. Lighting accounts for a third of the electricity use in the United States, more than half of which is generated by coal, the primary source of carbon dioxide emissions.

Powering a single incandescent bulb over its lifespan requires burning eighty-two pounds of coal, about one hundred times the amount needed to power a compact fluorescent. Analysts from Environmental Defense estimate that if every household replaced three 60-watt incandescent bulbs with compact fluorescents, the nation would reduce its greenhouse-gas emissions by an amount equivalent to taking 3.5 million cars off the highways. As of late 2007, 95 percent of Americans used incandescent bulbs. That is going to have to change in coming years, as the federal government plans to phase them out in the next few years.

Until other technologies such as better light-emitting diodes (LEDs) replace household lights, compact fluorescent bulbs are a great choice. They use one-third to one-fourth the electricity and last ten times as long as incandescent bulbs. And best of all, they can be used in standard bulb sockets, so you don't need to install new fixtures.

Compact fluorescents produce the same amount of light (measured in lumens, with one lumen equaling one candle's light), but they also don't cast that acid-like greenish hue they once did. My family has switched to compact fluorescents, and the lighting difference is negligible while the effect on the electric bill was immediate. They cast a warm light with no discernible flicker.

Warning: Don't throw used fluorescent bulbs in the regular trash. They contain mercury, a poison that can get into the food chain and continue to accumulate there. The mercury is sealed inside the bulb and is less than three milligrams, about the size of a ballpoint pen tip, while a power plant will emit ten milligrams of mercury to produce enough electricity to run an incandescent bulb. Wal-Mart has begun working with four major lightbulb manufacturers to reduce the amount of mercury in compact fluorescents by a third. Still, you must discard these bulbs as hazardous waste. Retailers are beginning to respond to this need: Home Depot has started a recycling program. Check with your city or town government, also.

Sources: Christine Woodside, "This Little Light of Mine," *Audubon* magazine, November–December 2007, pp. 92–96; the Worldwatch Institute's online guide to conservation at home, "Good Stuff," www.worldwatch.org/pubs/goodstuff; Jeff Deyette, energy analyst, the Union of Concerned Scientists in Boston, interview with the author, June 2005.

A Fraction of the Wattage

Incandescent wattage	Comparable compact fluorescent wattage
40	9
60	13
75	20
100	23
120	26

Choose a more efficient hot-water heater

The U.S. Department of Energy estimates that water heating accounts for 20 percent or more of an average household's annual energy expenditure. The yearly operating cost of a gas water heater is about $200; an electric costs about $450. Conserving hot water can be the single most important conservation step you take. Change the heater to a solar-powered one (see chapter 2). Limit shower lengths and install a low-flow showerhead, available from hardware stores and through some water companies. Buy a front-loading washing machine (see the section on clothes washers on page 124). Avoid rinsing dishes when loading a dishwasher; these machines are designed to handle some food on the dishes.

Source: U.S. Department of Energy, Energy Efficiency and Renewable Energy online fact sheets. See www.eere.energy.gov/consumer.

Wash dishes carefully

Should you wash dishes by hand or with a dishwasher? It depends on how you handle either. It's possible to waste hot water either way.

If washing by hand, here are some tips: Don't run the hot water every time you have a few dishes and don't leave the water running as you rakishly swipe at things with the sponge before moving the item back under the stream to rinse. Washing by hand can save water if you consolidate dishes and wash many at one time. I learned this technique from my mother-in-law, who serves meals for twenty in a cottage: Fill a tub with sudsy water, wash everything in proper sequence to maximize the suds. Start with silverware and then dishes that touched people's mouths, proceed next to bowls and plates, then wash the serving dishes, and finally, do the pots). Finally, rinse everything at once. Some people rinse in a clean tub of water, following the same sequence as for washing. Others run the water over each item, turning it off in between rinses. That can be tedious, but it provides a cleaner rinse.

If you aren't up to this routine, a low-energy dishwasher (so rated by the U.S. government's Energy Star labels) is the best choice. Run it on a short cycle. Don't wash the dishes twice by overrinsing before loading. Don't use the heated drying cycle. Open the door and let the dishes air-dry. If you have turned down your water heater to 120°F to save energy, as we have, but worry about sterilizing the dishes, as we have, many dishwashers offer an "energy boost" button. It uses more energy, but only for the dishes.

Sources: My years of hard-earned wisdom in the kitchen; "A Consumer's Guide to Energy Efficiency," U.S. Department of Energy's Energy Efficiency and Renewable Energy program, www.eere.energy.gov/consumer.

A bath or shower?

Because showers and baths account for about a quarter of a household's water use, this is an area where we must cut back. Short showers use less water than baths. Beware the trap of daydreaming in the shower, solving all of your problems as you create more for yourself, allowing excess hot water to run down the drain. Consider the following:

- Bathtub capacities range from 30 to 75 gallons.
- Older showerheads use 3.5 gallons per minute.
- Low-flow shower-heads use 2.5 gallons per minute or less.

Use this data to calculate the best way to save water. It's pretty clear that unless you like baths in a few inches of water, showers usually will save energy. Just divide the number of gallons in a bath by the number of gallons per minute your showerhead uses, and your answer will show how many minutes you would have to shower to fill the tub that high.

For instance, let's compare a low-flow showerhead to a modest thirty-gallon bath. As long as you take a shower that is shorter than twelve minutes, you will save water in the shower. No one should be taking a shower this long.

Source: Water Resources Research Center, College of Agriculture, University of Arizona, "Water in the Tucson Area: Seeking Sustainability," www.ag.arizona.edu.

Transportation

Leave the Car Home Once a Week

It's a simple act that can be like buying a lower-mileage car before you can afford it. Leave the car at home one out of five workdays. The boss might allow you to work at home one day; plenty do now. Or negotiate four ten-hour workdays. Or bicycle, take the bus, or walk to work.

Just how significant can this change be? If your commute is twenty miles one way and you get two weeks of vacation each year, at the end of one year you'd drive two thousand fewer miles, saving about eighty gallons of gas even if your car gets a measly but fairly typical twenty-five miles per gallon. Even if your commute is only a mile each way, you still save four gallons of gas, which equals a small bag of groceries. The American Automobile Association (AAA) makes the obvious point in a recent edition of its member magazine that carpooling to work saves money and major amounts of emissions. A group of four people who each used to drive alone cut emissions of the group by 75 percent.

Hypermiling: Change Your Driving Technique

Hypermilers, a group first identified in 2004, became folk heroes when gas prices jumped above $4 a gallon in 2008. That is because they have proven that individual action can save dramatic amounts of gasoline, carbon emissions, and money. How can anyone argue with this?

I recommend reading the primer at www.hypermiling.com. Their techniques range from the brilliant to the risky. I have devised my own list for the common person based on the hypermilers' ideas. All of these ideas below are legal as far as I know.

1. **Understand your car's gas mileage in order to realize the benefits of improving it.** Fill the tank and record the odometer reading or reset the trip odometer. When you next refill, record the number of gallons the tank took and record the odometer reading. Calculate how many miles you drove before this refilling. Take that distance and divide by the number of gallons you just put into the tank.

2. **Take a serious look at your behavior on the road.**
Many drivers are in a hurry and create all sorts of
troubles for themselves that use more gas. (Until
I began thinking about this, I was.) We feel other
drivers are holding us up, so we scold them by
tailgating or veering around them dramatically. We
follow other cars too closely and put energy into
braking and then accelerating back up to speed.
Numerous studies have concluded that speeding
does not get you to your destination more quickly,
within reason. One day I decided to putt-putt at
fifty-five miles per hour up the highway for about
ten miles; a car that had passed me two exits back
was sitting at the exit ramp light when I got off. I'm
no scientist, but I've watched this sort of thing happen often, whether I'm in the mood to be the slow
one or I'm the car that tried to save time by speeding and then got stuck.

3. **When you see a slowdown or traffic jam up ahead,
gradually slow down to maintain a wide space
between you and the car ahead of you.** Hypermilers cite as their inspiration for this idea a series of
articles by William Beaty, a chemistry professor at the
University of Washington, who experimented during his commute in the Seattle area, finding that the
best way to save gas and time is to drive the average speed of the traffic and allow other cars to merge
—rather than to rush ahead to "win" and not let anyone in. Such techniques can work on back roads. The
hypermilers advocate slowing down when you see
a red light ahead, taking your foot off the gas pedal

and coasting up to the light. The goal here is to avoid coming to a complete stop before the light turns green. This is fine if it works, but you can take it to unreasonable lengths, coasting down to ten miles per hour a distance before the light, and this might invite an accident. Just be careful.

4. **Accelerate smoothly.** Don't peel out or put the pedal to the metal. The hypermilers offer all sorts of techniques for doing this, such as allowing an automatic car to start on its own without the brake before you accelerate and driving barefoot to feel the pedal better. But driving barefoot is against the law in some states, and starting out slowly requires finesse without getting rear-ended, and so, be careful.

Sources: *The New York Times Week in Review*, "Buzzwords 2007: All We Are Saying," December 23, 2007; National Public Radio, "Car Gas Mileage May Not Be All It Seems," an interview with hypermilers, June 19, 2008; for Beaty's article about traffic waves, see http://amasci.com/amateur/traffic/trafexp.html.

Look Into Motor Scooters

Vespa and other companies manufacture these little motor bikes that are great for short commutes and get incredible gas mileage. But don't forget that they don't go fast enough for highways. So while they save gas, you must factor in that there will be many days you can't use them. It might be possible to sell your second car and share the first car with a family member, using the scooter for those short trips.

Avoid Burning Gas in Landscaping

Reel mowers, the nonmotorized circular blades that were common pre–World War II, don't use any fuel. Buy them at home stores and through catalogs. They are difficult to push when compared to a power mower, but they provide a good workout on a small lawn. Likewise, there is no need on a small residential plot to own gas-powered blowers or trimmers. Their noise alone would yield a noise citation in some cities.

Solaris makes this lawn mower with an option to run off a solar panel. New designs of this are expected to be on sale at Home Depot. (Photo courtesy of Linamar Consumer Products, Guelph, Ontario)

Surveying Energy Use at Home

Electricity

Gather electric bills for the past year. Utilities can provide copies of bills, or printouts of several months' use, on request. Record the kilowatt-hours (recorded as "kWh" on bills) your house or apartment used on a month-by-month basis. Then add the total for the year.

Month	kWh
Total kWh =	

To learn the impact of each resident of your house, divide your total kilowatt-hour figure by the number of residents.

Per capita electricity use = _____ kWh.

Next you must calculate how much fuel your utility burned to provide your electricity. The figures in the calculations below were devised by Peter Markow, a professor at St. Joseph's College in West Hartford, Connecticut, based upon actual data from power sources in the northeastern United States.

Nuclear power plant

Consumes 0.0005 uranium fuel pellet per kWh.

To determine how many uranium fuel pellets are needed for your house, multiply 0.44 x your total kWh x 0.0005:

0.44 x _____ kWh x 0.0005 pellets/kWh

0.44 x _____ x 0.0005 = _____ uranium fuel pellets

Oil-burning power plant

Burns 0.066 gallon per kWh.

To determine how many gallons of #6 fuel oil are needed for your house, multiply 0.29 x your total kWh x 0.066:

0.29 x _____ kWh x 0.066 = _____ gallons #6 fuel oil

Coal-burning power plant

Burns 0.78 pound of coal per kWh.

To determine how many pounds of coal are needed for your house, multiply 0.05 x your total kWh x 0.78:

0.05 x _____ kWh x 0.78 = _____ pounds of coal

Trash-to-energy plant

Burns 3.5 pounds of trash per kWh.

To determine how many pounds of garbage must be burned to provide electricity for your house, multiply 0.08 x your total kWh x 3.5:

0.08 x _____ kWh x 3.5 = _____ pounds of garbage

Heat

Home Heating Oil

Find your home heating bills for the past year and determine the number of gallons used at your house. Divide by the number of people in your house to determine your annual use of home heating oil.

Date	Gallons	Date	Gallons

Total gallons = _____
gallons/person = _____

Liquefied Propane or Natural Gas

Find your home gas bills for the past year and determine the number of pounds, cubic meters, or other unit of measure recorded on them. Divide the total gas used by the number of residents in your house or apartment to determine your annual use of natural gas.

Date	Lbs or cubic meters	Date	Lbs or cubic meters

Total lbs or cubic meters = _____
lbs or cubic meters/person = _____

Car Gasoline

To figure how much gasoline you burned driving, determine the total number of miles you have driven your car in the past year.

Then divide the total miles driven by your average miles per gallon for your car.

_____ miles driven in the last year divided by _____ mpg (your car's average) = _____ gallons you burned.

Source: Peter Markow, Saint Joseph College, West Hartford, Connecticut

CHAPTER TEN

An Appliance Manifesto

There is a specter haunting North America, and it just might be the fleet of electric appliances crowding our houses and apartments. Which appliance is bad and extraneous? That is a difficult question. For one family it might be the freestanding freezer, sucking up about one-eighth of one family's electric bill while they forget about the heaps of frozen meat hidden within. Or it might be the clothes dryer, running too hot and too long, costing hundreds of dollars a year. Whatever it may be, I now present my manifesto for each citizen to get rid of several appliances. While I suggest a list here, I can't force you to choose these particular gadgets. Perhaps you'll be inspired to find others. The only criterion is that they use electricity to perform tasks that could be handled without electricity.

In 1964 my parents took me and my three brothers to the World's Fair in New York. I was five years old. The General Electric (GE) home show so captivated me that I refused to leave the auditorium to go to the ladies' room. My parents liked to repeat this story of their little daughter who would let nothing stop her from watching the entire home show with its life-size dioramas of the American kitchen from the 1890s through the 1960s. Walt Disney himself created this show. Each period kitchen took up a segment of a circular stage. The audience revolved around the stage several degrees for each act, depicting a new era roughly twenty years later than the previous one. Mechanized mannequins chatted about their appliances and lights as they looked out at the audience. All of the kitchens seemed homey, although each looked sleeker than the last.

When the home show moved to Disneyland as "Progress-land" a few years after the World's Fair, it added a final act set in the near future—meaning in the late 1960s—in which a family ambled through an indoor mall near a nuclear power plant. The mannequins in this new scene discussed the wonders of inexpensive and clean energy. Here is a snippet of dialogue from that last act:

> **Mother:** Today our whole downtown is completely enclosed. Whatever the weather is outside, it's always dry and comfortable inside.
>
> **Father:** General Electric calls it a climate-controlled environment. But Mother calls it . . .
>
> **Mother:** A sparkling jewel. Now far off to your right, we have a welcome neighbor . . .
>
> **Father:** Our GE nuclear power plant, dear.[1]

To my parents and their peers, progress in this postmodern world, after World War II, meant that everyday life no longer involved heavy labor. Everyone, even a five-year-old girl, could understand the comforts and promise in new technology. I think of the early 1960s as one of the most hopeful times in modern American history. Home appliances had wrought a sea change in home routines. Jet travel and space exploration were becoming everyday events. But traditional social mores had not yet begun to unravel. In this era, sometimes called the postmodern era, people placed an uncomplicated faith in the new comforts. There was a feeling that our parents deserved them after the hard years of the Depression and World War II.

A lot has happened since then. The Vietnam War; the back-to-the-land movement; the disco era; the energy crisis; the "Reagan Revolution"; the first Iraq war; the dot-com boom; the global-warming controversy; the events of September 11, 2001; the second war in Iraq. . . . Today might well be called the post-postmodern era. The optimism of the GE home show in 1964 is gone. Energy isn't plentiful or cheap anymore. We're humbled by the failure of the nuclear age to live up to its promises. We worry about the still-expanding world population's strain on the planet's resources.

My ideal post-postmodern version of the General Electric Progressland would include a new diorama for the early twenty-first century. Instead of symbols of plentiful energy, today's kitchen scene might bear some resemblance to the Great Depression, not in its technology or looks, but in the restraint we'll begin to exercise there. We are on the verge of a time when typical Americans no longer bask in the convenience but must tally the energy burning. My new act would include the following dialogue:

> **Father:** Our parents thought that nuclear fusion would create cheap and limitless electricity. Today we know that hasn't come true. We're practicing energy conservation right here at home—Mom got rid of the extra television, the freestanding freezer, and the extra fridge that held the soda and beer.

> **Mother:** We don't even miss them! What were we thinking?

Lighting, cooking, and appliances use 33 percent of the energy in a typical home, according to the U.S. Department of Energy. Many appliances have become greatly efficient, particularly the major workhorses like the refrigerator, clothes washer, and dishwasher. To compare new models of these to their counterparts of a decade ago shows a major savings in energy. But we continue to use more power! The Michigan-based Consumers Energy, one of the largest utility companies in the nation, has found that for the past two decades, the average increase in power use per household has been 1 percent a year.[2] Emissions in the United States rose by more than 16 percent between 1990 and 2005, according to a report by the U.S. Environmental Protection Agency, which assigns much of the blame to rising electricity demands.[3]

Electricity consumption has been rising steadily for the last dozen years because of an increasing population and new objects like bigger televisions, and it's projected to rise nearly 2 percent in 2009. Each person in America, at home, has used about the same amount of energy as in 1990, and this is expected to continue, more or less, until 2030 if we continue to use the same appliances and heating and cooling methods. But if we improve our technology, home energy use per person could take a drastic nosedive. And that would be about time, considering how much energy we consume in the United States to begin with. Energy intensity—energy use per $2,000 of gross domestic product—declines every year, so the reason why energy consumption doesn't is this: We're using ever more energy, per person, all the time.[4]

So what about it? How could we do so poorly when we know so much? It could be that until recently electricity and fuel weren't very expensive, so it didn't really matter. Prices are jumping off our previous charts now. Now is the time to turn our attention to the whole second category of appliances—the unnecessary.

One way to figure out which appliances you can discard is to consider the advice of emergency preparedness experts, who often recommend unplugging unnecessary appliances when the forecast is for thunder and lightning. Anything you can do without before a storm deserves closer scrutiny. Many—not all—of the things you'd unplug in a crisis are expendable appliances at other times, also. Some appliances are always expendable. Which ones you can ditch depends somewhat on your particular lifestyle and locale. Consider dispensing with the appliances listed below. Under each one I've estimated the typical amount of energy a household would need and converted it to kilowatt-hours. The financial cost here is not the cost of buying each appliance but only the cost of the electricity to run it. Clearly, you have to take the initial cost of the appliance into account too.

Freestanding freezer, 345 watts
Environmental cost: 1,007 kilowatt-hours a year
Annual financial cost: $101 to $181

Our 345-watt freestanding freezer seemed the perfect money-saving solution. We'd buy bargain food and freeze it. We'd save more money than it cost to run the freezer. Assuming it actually runs for about eight hours out of every twenty-four, the environmental cost of this freezer is 2.76 kilowatt-hours each day, or 1,007 kilowatt hours per year. At the rate of electricity at that time—14.5 cents per kilowatt-hour—we were paying $146 a year to store food. If we still had it, we'd be paying $181. Even at a typical lower rate found throughout much of the United

States, 10 cents per kilowatt-hour, the freezer would still cost $101 a year to run.

Financially you could justify this. All a shopper has to save is a few dollars a week on food that could be frozen for later use. I used to think that for us, storing food saved not only money but also energy—energy in the form of gas saved by making fewer trips to the store. But this isn't true for us. We live near the center of our town, a half a mile from the local supermarket. We live eighteen miles from the discount big-box supermarket where I used to search for most of the frozen bargains. Each trip to that wholesale store now costs several dollars in gas. Then we pay more to store it for months on end. This freezer isn't worth it for us unless I begin shopping much more efficiently for bargains, thereby reducing the number of car trips to the store. With our supermarket so close by, that will take some doing. I have a friend who freezes her garden produce and who diligently stockpiles bargains in the freezer. For her family the freezer deserves to stay.

Clothes dryer, 3,400 watts

Environmental cost: 1,862 kilowatt-hours a year

Annual financial cost: $186 to $335

These figures assume the dryer handles ten loads a week, or two loads on each of five days. This means that each load costs from 36 to about 65 cents. Even if you like to pay hundreds of dollars for something a line or rack provides for nothing (minus the cost of the line or rack), there is no way a household could switch to solar or wind power and consume this many kilowatt-hours per year just for drying clothes.

I do feel guilty criticizing the dryer, which my own mother said so changed her life that she would never go back. She has described scenes of chaos with the wet clothes in her

Philadelphia backyard in the 1940s. The wooden clothesline props would routinely slip, dragging the wet fabric into the wet grass. Or it would start raining and she, her sisters, and her mother would run outside and scramble to take the clothes in. I don't blame her for loving her dryer.

And yet dryers gobble energy. The viable alternative to dryers—hanging clothes to dry—uses no energy but adds fifteen minutes to your time (per load). In times like these the dryer must fall under new scrutiny. Someone could invent better clothes-hanging devices than sagging ropes and rickety clothes props.

Revisit this time-honored method of drying clothes. The energy is free. Hanging one load takes about 15 minutes. (Photo courtesy of author)

An antidryer movement, Right to Dry, has sprung up in Concord, New Hampshire. Its founder gives speeches and provides statistics to some of the harder audiences—people who live in gated communities where clotheslines aren't allowed, or older people who grew up with clotheslines and are tired of them.

Microwave oven, 1,000 watts

Environmental cost: 183 kilowatt-hours a year

Annual financial cost: $18.30 to $32.90

At the risk of sounding like a barbarian, I contend that no one needs to own a microwave oven, even though it uses less energy than most regular ovens. I have assumed that the microwave runs for a half an hour a day, all year. Most of what a microwave does well requires no extra source of electricity at all. Microwaves reheat drinks that could stay warm in an insulated jug. Microwaves defrost food that could defrost in the refrigerator over a few hours. Microwaves heat mediocre premade meals. The main problem, though, is that no matter how efficient a microwave may be, it cannot completely replace a regular oven. It can't brown or broil anything, for instance. You will still use your regular oven, perhaps even while you are running the microwave.

If you must own a microwave, at least be honest about its place in the kitchen. It is a convenience, not an energy saver.

Garbage disposal, 800 watts

Environmental cost: 21 kilowatt-hours a year

Annual financial cost: A few dollars

It's not easy to stand up against something that costs so little to operate, but garbage disposals are not necessary in any but the most cramped urban conditions. Out of the city, you can compost the garbage for free.

Electric blanket, 100 watts

Environmental cost: 74 kilowatt-hours a year

Annual financial cost: $7.40 to $13.32

A double-size 100-watt electric blanket seems harmless. But you might use this for eight hours a night for the three coldest months of the year, consuming 74 kilowatt-hours a year. This is a pure luxury item. The only way you could justify it otherwise is if you had no heat in the house.

Hair dryer

Environmental cost: 78 kilowatt-hours a year

Annual financial cost: $7.80 to $14.04

I admit I don't fuss with my hair. Therefore I can't see spending fifteen minutes a day holding one of these heated monsters. Hair dryers do the job fast, but the alternative, air drying, uses no electricity at all. The question to ask yourself is this: What does a hair dryer provide, and is it worth paying and using energy for this? The benefits might be that a hair dryer saves some embarrassment in public, since you don't have to go out with a wet head.

Trash compactor, 1,500 watts

Environmental cost: 113 kilowatt-hours a year

Annual financial cost: $11.30 to $20.34

Here, I assume the compactor runs for fifteen minutes a day on three hundred days of the year. Compactors, invented in the 1970s, make sense only if space is an issue. Where I live, our trash is incinerated, so there's little point in compacting it. At a large office building, school, or factory, using a commercial compactor could save maintenance workers' time emptying trash bins. At home you'd be better off reducing what you throw in the trash.

Electric can opener, 175 watts

Environmental cost: Only the cost of manufacturing it.

Annual financial cost: Pennies

I include the electric can opener as a symbol of the unnecessary. These things make a tremendous amount of noise and take up room in the kitchen. What's the point of owning one, unless for health reasons you can't operate a manual can opener?

One appliance about which I've changed my mind . . .

Toaster Oven (1,100 watts) or Toaster (1,200 watts)
A toaster oven uses one-third to a half as much energy as a conventional-size oven. Baking something small in a toaster oven clearly saves energy. A toaster oven also uses about the same amount of power as a regular toaster. If you use either of these to toast bread, the amount of time the appliance runs costs only pennies a day.[5]

It might seem crazy to talk about electric can openers and blankets when there's a war on. But in a sense this is an exercise— the most important one you can do as an individual, to think about starting a revolution in your house or apartment. The truth is, we know too much now not to do this. We know too much about how energy use accelerates the well-documented warming of the world's average temperature. We know that our habits affect the health of the planet. The most logical reason that we wouldn't act on what we know now, I think, is that we live with dozens more appliances than we had in 1964. Our residential infrastructure is out of control. This is fairly easy to change.

Consumers of the world, unite. You have nothing to lose but your kilowatt-hours.

Appendix:
Where to Learn More

General Information about Energy, Consumption, and Alternatives

U.S. Energy Information Administration, www.eia.doe.gov
This site has more statistics than you might ever have time to read.

U.S. Department of Energy's Office of Energy Efficiency and Renewable Energy, www.eere.energy.gov
Peruse this site for many fact sheets and descriptions of technology for citizens.

The National Renewable Energy Lab
Part of the U.S. Department of Energy, this lab began in the 1970s as the Solar Research Institute. Its main offices in Golden, Colorado, are the headquarters of divisions covering solar energy, wind energy, and biomass. The labs also study energy efficiency, hybrid-car technology, geothermal technology, and how to integrate alternative energy into national policies. The NREL Visitor Center is located at 15013 Denver West Parkway, Golden, Colorado 80401-3393. For information call (303) 384-6565, or go to www.nrel.gov.

The Database of State Incentives for Renewable Energy, www.dsireusa.org

This site lists rebates, loans, and other incentives for dozens of renewable energy or energy-efficient projects. You may search this database by the type of energy you are considering or simply look at a chart showing every kind of incentive available for your state. No matter where you live, you will be able to use a federal tax credit for many energy efficient installations and many renewable projects. You will be surprised at how much money you can save on many projects, from storm windows to wind turbines. Check it out!

American Council for an Energy-Efficient Economy (ACEEE)

1001 Connecticut Avenue, NW, Suite 801

Washington, DC 20036

(202) 429-8873

or

2140 Shattuck Avenue, Suite 202

Berkeley, CA 94704

ACEEE provides general and technical information on energy efficiency, including these publications: *The Consumer Guide to Home Energy Savings, The Most Energy-Efficient Appliances,* and *Saving Energy and Money with Home Appliances.* They can be ordered by writing the ACEEE office in Berkeley.

California Energy Commission, www.energy.ca.gov

To reach the commission's Renewable Energy & Consumer Energy Efficiency Information line, call toll-free in California, (800) 555-7794; outside California, (916) 654-4058.

Storey's Basic Country Skills: A Practical Guide to Self-Reliance

John and Martha Storey, Pownal, VT: Storey Books, 1991.

This book offers good, basic discussions of skills needed to save energy, heat with wood, and insulate the house.

Periodicals

These days any business section or consumer magazine offers nearly daily reports of oil supplies and prices, the growth of the alternative energy industry, pollution, consumption, and research. These three go beyond the general to explain the technology of alternative energy in clear language.

Home Power
P.O. Box 520
Ashland, OR 97520
This bimonthly magazine offers practical articles for laypeople on using renewable energy at home. For subscription information go to www.homepower.com/magazine.

Mother Earth News
Ogden Publications, Inc.
1503 SW 42nd Street
Topeka, KS 66609-1265
This is a bimonthly magazine on self-sufficient living. To subscribe call (800) 234-3369, or go to www.motherearthnews .com.

Wired
660 Third Street
San Francisco, CA 94107
This monthly magazine covers all aspects of new technology, including alternative vehicles. To subscribe call (800) SOWIRED

or (303) 678-0354, send an e-mail to subscriptions@wiredmag
.com, or go to www.wiredmag.com.

Chapter 1—The Situation Today: Oil Still Rules

Energy Bulletin
This compendium of information about the world oil supply
reprints U.S. Rep. Roscoe Bartlett's presentation on March 14,
2005 at www.energybulletin.net/4733.htm.

American Association for the Study of Peak Oil and Gas
Box 25182, SE-750 25
Uppsala, Sweden
You can contact this organization of European scientists at the
address above, or visit www.peakoil.net.

U.S. Energy Information Administration
You can find the article, "Crude Oil and Total Petroleum Imports
Top 15 Countries," at www.eia.doe.gov/pub/oil_gas/petroleum/
data_publications/company_level_imports/current/import.html.

Lives Per Gallon: The True Cost of Our Oil Addiction by Terry
Tamminen, Washington, DC: Island Press/Shearwater Books,
2006.
This book by Terry Tamminen, an environmentalist and special
adviser to the governor of California, makes the case that the
country's dependence on oil threatens the globe's future and
has already damaged people's health, in addition to the other
problems related to high demand and finite supply.

Chapter 2—Demystifying Solar Energy

Findsolar.com, an online solar calculator.
The site is a consortium of the American Solar Energy Society, the Solar Electric Power Association, Energy Matters LLC, and the U.S. Department of Energy and its office of Energy Efficiency and Renewable Energy. The site's calculator will estimate the cost, power usage, payback times, and more of both solar hot-water systems and solar photovoltaic systems. As a result of my visit to this site, I've decided we can't wait to trim the top of the tree in the backyard and install that solar hot-water system on the roof. One of the points they make is that these systems increase property values in addition to saving fossil fuel–driven energy.

Finding a Solar Dealer
There are hundreds of solar dealers in the United States and elsewhere. For the most current list, contact your state government or write to:

    Solarbuzz USA
    P.O. Box 475815
    San Francisco, CA 94147-5815

    You can also call (415) 928-9743, send an e-mail to info@ solarbuzz.com, or go to www.solarbuzz.com and click on "Products."

State governments in thirty states offer rebate or incentive programs to buy solar panels as of April 2008. For an up-to-date list of programs, contact your state government, or view a detailed list published by the Database of State Incentives for Renewable Energy at www.dsireusa.org. This database is comprehensive and continually updated. The number and type of incentives may surprise you. Solar power isn't as shockingly expensive as many people think because of the high prices of electricity and fuel now.

Gail Burrington provided data and background on appliances and systems. Contact her at:

Burrington's Solar Edge

6 Reed Circle

Windsor Locks, CT 06096

(860) 623-0159

www.solaredge.biz

The Solar Energy Industries Association

805 15th Street NW

Washington, DC 20005

(202) 682-0556

www.seia.org

This trade organization in Washington, D.C., speaks for the industry and gives out information for potential buyers.

The Consortium for Advanced Residential Buildings (CARB)

Michael J. Crosbie

Steven Winter Associates, Inc.

50 Washington Street

Norwalk, CT 06854

This coalition of house designers and builders and product manufacturers is working with the U.S. Department of Energy to develop energy-efficient building techniques for new houses. To read the newsletter go to www.carb-swa.com/carb news-archive.html.

"Selecting a New Water Heater"

For information on solar water heaters, this booklet from the Energy Efficiency and Renewable Energy Clearinghouse of the National Renewable Energy Lab is helpful, although it was published in 1995.

Solar Roofing Shingles

I can't recommend specific brands of solar roofing shingles, but for more information about shingles that double as solar panels, consult Kyocera Solar, Inc., which makes a residential roof system called MyGen Meridian. For details go to the Kyocera Web site at www.kyocerasolar.com/products/meridian.html. Or consult United Solar Ovonic of Auburn Hills, Michigan, which makes a kind of solar panel that resembles a roll of plastic. The material is available as shingles, or it can cover metal roofs and awnings. For details go to www.uni-solar.com.

Direct-Current Solar Appliances

Another way to start small is to invest in solar-powered appliances, each attached to individual solar panels that send direct current to the appliance. (No inverter to convert to alternating current is necessary, because these don't connect to the household electrical system.) One of the most logical and useful solar-powered appliances is the solar-powered attic fan, also called an attic vent. It looks like a rectangular solar panel on the roof, but it includes a fan that blows hot air out of the house. The fan receives the most power from the solar unit during the time the house needs the fan the most—on hot, sunny days. These fans typically cost hundreds of dollars. Or try a solar-powered sump pump that won't have to rely on the electricity supply of the house, which might shut down during a flood. Individual solar panels hook up to power laptop computers and other communication devices for field work or travel. Call any solar dealer to ask about these products, or search the Web to learn more. Direct-current solar appliances even turn up on the Web auction site, eBay.

Chapter 3—Wind Generators at Home

The American Wind Energy Association (AWEA)
122 C Street NW, Suite 380
Washington, DC 20001
(202) 383-2500
www.awea.org
AWEA is a trade association based in Washington, D.C. It offers much information about wind power on a small scale and a utility scale, and periodically issues opinions on government policies and reports.

California Energy Commission Buydown Program
1516 Ninth Street
Sacramento, CA 95814
(916) 654-4058
www.consumerenergycenter.org/buydown/index.html
For California residents, rebates for wind projects are available to California residents through this program. Contact them for more information.

Buying a Small Wind Electric System: A California Consumer's Guide, Sacramento: California Energy Commission, 2002.
This publication can be downloaded from www.energy.ca.gov/renewables/documents/education_documents.html#materials

Consumer Energy Center of the California Energy Commission
1516 Ninth Street
Sacramento, CA 95814-5504
(916) 654-4287
renewable@energy.state.ca.us
www.consumerenergycenter.org

Contact this organization for a list of small wind turbines and dealers in California.

National Wind Technology Center
This program of the federal government is located at the National Renewable Energy Center outside Boulder, Colorado. For more information visit www.nrel.gov/wind.

"Apples and Oranges: Choosing a Home-Sized Wind Generator," by Mick Sagrillo, *Home Power,* No. 90, August–September 2002, p. 50.
This article provides general information on choosing a wind generator.

"Small Wind Systems," in the online guide "A Consumer's Guide to Energy Efficiency and Renewable Energy," by the U.S. Department of Energy, www.eere.energy.gov/consumer/your_home/electricity/index.cfm/mytopic=10880.
This chapter will give you details about weighing the advantages of your property and choosing a small wind system.

Chapter 4—Other Technologies: Fuel Cells, Biodiesel Fuel, and Geothermal Heat Pumps

International Association for Hydrogen Energy, www.iahe.org

Hydrogen Energy Center, www.h2eco.org

Biodiesel Power by Lyle Estill, Gabriola Island, BC, Canada: New Society Publishers, 2005.
For some background on the biodiesel movement, read this book by Piedmont Biofuels vice president Lyle Estill.

Biodiesel

This trade magazine is geared mainly to large-scale producers that can offer insight into this growing field.

International Ground Source Heat Pump Association (IGSHPA), www.igshpa.okstate.edu

Geothermal Heat Pump Consortium, www.geoexchange.org

U.S. Department of Energy guide to heat pumps, eere.energy .gov/consumer/your_home/space_heating_cooling/index.cfm/ mytopic=R640

Chapter 5—Heating with Wood

To locate retailers of woodstoves and heaters, contact:
Hearth, Patio & Barbecue Association
1601 North Kent Street, Suite 1001
Arlington, VA 22209
(703) 522-0086
www.hpba.org

"Burn It Smart," www.burnitsmart.org
Natural Resources Canada of Ottawa, Ontario, operates a Web site that offers this tutorial on woodstove use.

The U.S. Department of Energy's National Renewable Energy Laboratory recommends:

• *Chimney Safety Institute of America,* www.csia.org
This site will tell you how to safely vent a woodstove.

- *Hearth Education Foundation*, www.heartheducation.org
Visit this site to learn more about installing and using woodstoves.
- *Wood Heat*, www.woodheat.org
This Canadian nonprofit organization teaches responsible use of wood at home.

The Chimney Safety Institute of America
2155 Commercial Drive
Plainfield, IN 46168
(317)837-5362
www.csia.org
The institute provides a national listing of certified chimney sweeps and information on chimneys and venting combustion appliances.

U.S. Environmental Protection Agency Indoor Air Quality Information Clearinghouse, www.epa.gov/iaq/iaqxline.html
Visit this site for publications on indoor air quality, including those concerning wood heating.

EPA Wood Heater Program, www.epa.gov/
This program certifies wood-heating appliances and provides information on wood heating. Visit the Web site and click on "Compliance" and then "Wood Heater Program."

Hearth Education Foundation, www.heartheducation.org
This nonprofit organization teaches the public and profession-als about installing and using wood-burning appliances.

Masonry Heater Association of North America

1252 Stock Farm Road, Randolph, VT 05060

(802) 728-5896

www.mha-net.org

Chapter 6—Harnessing a Backyard Stream: Micro-Hydroelectric Systems

National Hydropower Association, www.hydro.org

Idaho National Engineering and Environmental Laboratory, http://hydropower.id.doe.gov/resourceassessment/states .shtml

United States Society on Dams

1616 Seventeenth Street, #483, Denver, Colorado 80202

(303) 628-5430 (phone)

(303) 628-5431 (fax)

stephens@ussdams.org

Chapter 7—Alternative Cars

Edmunds.com, www.edmunds.com

This Web-based magazine independently rates cars and trucks.

Transportation Energy Data Book, Edition 27, by Stacy C. Davis and Susan W. Diegel, Knoxville, TN: Oak Ridge National Laboratory, 2008.

You can download this book from http://cta.ornl.gov/data/ index.shtml.

Energy Information Administration, www.eia.doe.gov/steo
To help citizens keep up on gas prices, this arm of the U.S. Department of Energy issues short-term outlooks for energy prices, including car gasoline. Every month their estimates can change.

Chapter 8—Conservation: Not a New Idea

Energy Efficiency and Renewable Energy Program of the U.S. Department of Energy, www.eere.energy.gov/consumerinfo/factsheets.html.
For numerous fact sheets about alternative energy visit this Web site.

See also ***Energy Savers: Tips on Saving Money and Energy at Home,*** www1.eere.energy.gov/consumer/tips/.

Consumer Guide to Home Energy Savings by Alex Wilson, Jennifer Thorne, and John Morrill, Washington, DC: American Council for an Energy-Efficient Economy, 2003.

Natural Resources Defense Council, (212) 727-2700; www.nrdc.org
This New York–based advocacy and lobbying organization produces consumer guides to energy conservation.

Chapter 9—Conservation Tips

For general information
U.S. Department of Energy's Energy Efficiency and Renewable Energy Clearinghouse
(800) DOE-3732
www.eere.energy.gov/buildings/homes/insulatinghome.cfm

Energy Savers: Tips on Saving Energy & Money at Home,
www1.eere.energy.gov/consumer/tips/
This is a thirty-six-page booklet produced by the U.S. Department of Energy, Energy Efficiency and Renewable Energy Department.

No-Electricity Gadgets

Manual coffee grinder
Reasonably priced at the Overstocked Kitchen. See www.over stockedkitchen.zoovy.com/product/OM-CGNDR?meta=FRG.

Windup Radios and Flashlights
Innovative Technologies sells hand-powered necessities invented by Trevor Baylis. Call (888) 322-1455, or go to www .windupradio.com. L.L. Bean manufactures its own versions.

Reel lawn mowers
A throwback to the early twentieth century, these contraptions, when pushed, roll a reel comprised of curved blades over the grass. Available through some catalogs and chain stores like Home Depot.

Solar Shower Bags

Camping and boating devices allow you to hang a bag of water in the sun. When heated, you stand beneath it and open the valve. It's a short shower, but effective. For one model, see the Raytech catalog at www.raytechcatalog.com.

Chapter 10—An Appliance Manifesto

The federal Energy Information Administration compiles reports on people's use of electricity and appliances at home. The administration is a program of the U.S. Department of Energy in Washington, D.C. To read the reports, press releases, and other data, go to www.eia.doe.gov.

Notes

To ensure that readers may easily locate Web-based articles that may have been moved around a site, for some of the links I have listed the home page, from which the article can be found by using the site's search engine.

Introduction—Why You Need this Book

1. Intergovernmental Panel on Climate Change, "Climate Change 2007: Synthesis Report," a summary of the IPCC findings of its Fourth Assessment Report, Valencia, Spain: November 12–17, 2007, 30–38.

2. Let's not forget that the United States refused to sign an international treaty, the Kyoto Protocol, in 2001, when many developed countries did sign. Europe has taken steps to regulate carbon emissions. The United States has insisted—understandably—that world energy agreements should be fair. But it has been slow to act. Now the banking industry, power company leaders, and the corporate world have said some sort of regulation of carbon emissions is necessary. For more information see www.yaleclimatemediaforum.org.

3. www.inflationdata.com/inflation/Inflation_Rate/Gasoline_Inflation.asp.

Chapter 1—The Situation Today: Oil Still Rules

1. United States Energy Information Administration, www.eia .gov. Information also available on the Conoco Phillips Web site, www.conocophillips.com/newsroom/other_resources/energy answers/future_supply.htm.

2. David Deming, "Are We Running Out of Oil?" a "Policy Backgrounder" article of the National Center for Policy Analysis, www.ncpa.org/pub/bg/bg159/index.html#c. Deming writes, "By the year 2000, a total of 900 billion barrels of oil had been produced. Total world oil production in 2000 was 25 billion barrels. If world oil consumption continues to increase at an average rate of 1.4 percent a year, and no further resources are discovered, the world's oil supply will not be exhausted until the year 2056."

3. John M. Broder, "Bush Signs Broad Energy Bill," *The New York Times,* December 19, 2007. Fred Sissine, "Energy Independence and Security Act of 2007: A Summary of the Major Provisions." Washington, D.C.: Congressional Research Service, December 21, 2007.

4. James A. Fay and Dan S. Golumb, *Energy and the Environment,* (New York: Oxford University Press, 2002), 23. Clifford Krauss, "U.S. Coal's Global Appeal: Exports Are Rising, And So Is the Price," *The New York Times,* March 19, 2008, first business page.

5. "Back to black," *New Scientist,* November 10, 2007, 4.

6. U.S. Energy Information Administration of the U.S. Department of Energy, www.eia.doe.gov. This refers to data showing that 40 percent of the U.S. energy sources come from petroleum.

7. Web site of the Society of Petroleum Engineers of Richardson, Texas, www.spe.org.

8. United States Energy Information Administration, Annual Energy Review 2006, page xx.

9. PFC Energy, "PFC Energy's Global Crude Oil and Natural Gas Liquids Supply Forecast" (PowerPoint presentation), Washington, D.C., September 2004; cited in Stark, Linda, editor, Worldwatch Institute, *Vital Signs 2005,* (New York: Norton, 2005), 30.

10. Energy experts, writers, and the U.S. Department of Energy all have described the peak oil concept. U.S. Rep. Roscoe Bartlett of Maryland went into detail about it in a presentation he gave in March 2005 to the U.S. House of Representatives.

11. "ExxonMobil 2007 Summary Annual Report," Irving Texas, 8 and 20–22.

12. See www.theoildrum.com/node/3839. Also, Fay and Golumb, *Energy and the Environment,* 25. Concise description of the oil shale reserves.

13. Energy briefing on the United States, U.S. Department of Energy, Energy Information Administration, www.eia.doe.gov/emeu/cabs/usa.html.

14. Fay and Golumb, *Energy and the Environment,* 23.

15. Bruce Murray, "Assessing the East Coast Blackout: Was Deregulation to Blame?" Facsnet.org, August 19, 2003, www.facsnet.org/tools/energy/blackout.php. Severin Borenstein, professor of business administration and public policy at the University of California, Berkeley, is quoted in this article. Also, Associated Press wire service, "How the Power Grid System Works," August 14, 2003.

16. U.S.-Canada Power System Outage Task Force, "Final Report on the August 14, 2003, Blackout in the United States and Canada: Causes and Recommendations," April 2004, available online from the Harvard Electricity Policy Group, www.ksg.harvard.edu.

17. Thomas L. Friedman, speech at Brown University reported by the author, April 22, 2008.

18. "Interview with James Kunstler," *High Country News,* June 13, 2005, 13. See also Kunstler's books, *The Long Emergency: Surviving the Converging Catastrophes of the Twenty-first Century* (New York: Atlantic Monthly Press, 2005) and earlier titles, *Geography of Nowhere: The Rise and Decline of America's Man-Made Landscape* (New York: Touchstone, 1994) and *Home From Nowhere: Remaking Our Everyday World,* (New York: Touchstone, 1996).

19. "Parties Split on How to Expand Offshore Drilling," *The New York Times,* June 6, 2008.

Chapter 2—Demystifying Solar Energy

1. Jimmy Carter, "The President's Proposed Energy Policy" (televised speech, April 18, 1977), *Vital Speeches of the Day,* 43, no. 14 (May 1, 1977), 418–20. Available online at www.pbs.org/wgbh/amex/carter/filmmore/ps_energy.html.

2. Peter Marbach, former development director at Unity College, and other staffers at Unity College, solar installers, and others, telephone interviews with the author, 1997 through 2005.

3. Most of these facts come from the CIA *World Factbook,* a compilation of government statistics (see www.cia.gov). My source here is NationMaster.com, a Web site that compiles statistics on many countries.

4. Mark Gielecki, Fred Mayes, and Lawrence Prete, "Incentives, Mandates, and Government Programs for Promoting Renewable Energy," U.S. Energy Information Administration of the U.S. Department of Energy, www.eia.doe.gov/cneaf/solar.renewables/rea_issues/incent.html. The federal government

offered homeowners tax credits of 30 percent of the first $2,000 and 20 percent of the next $8,000 for solar and wind equipment. In 1980 the incentives increased to 30 percent to 40 percent of the first $10,000 and added geothermal technology to the equipment covered. By 1985 the government had stopped offering the credits.

5. Janet L. Sawin, "Solar Energy Markets Booming," *Vital Signs 2005,* 36.

6. Janet L. Sawin, "Another Sunny Year for Solar Power," *Vital Signs Online,* Worldwatch Institute, 2007.

7. Rebecca Smith, "Shareholder Scorecard: Best 1-Year Performer: First Solar." *Wall Street Journal,* February 25, 2008.

8. Ed Witkin of Bridgewater, Connecticut, interview with the author, March 2005. Also, *Solar Today* (online), July-August, www. solartoday.org/2008/july_august08/paying_for_it.htm.

9. Anthony DePalma, "New Jersey Dealing with Solar Policy's Success," *The New York Times,* June 25, 2008

10. Gail Burrington, owner of Burrington's Solar Edge, Windsor, Connecticut, telephone interview with the author, March 2005.

11. *Connecticut Consumer's Guide to Buying a Solar Electric System* (Rocky Hill: Connecticut Clean Energy Fund), 3. This is based on a guide by Tom Starrs and Howard Wenger for the California Energy Commission with the National Renewable Energy Laboratory, Golden, Colorado.

12. Michael J. Crosbie, "Cutting the Power," CARBNews (vol. 8, no. 9, March 2005), the newsletter of the Consortium for Advanced Residential Buildings, a project of the Building America Program sponsored partly by the U.S. Department of Energy. CARBNews is published by Steven Winter Associates of Norwalk, Connecticut, www.carb-swa.com/carb news-archive.html.

13. Peter Markow, Tolland, Connecticut, interview with the author, April 2005.

Chapter 3—Wind Generators at Home

1. Michael T. Eckhart, "Renewable Energy 2005: A Mid-Year Review," www.renewableenergyaccess.com. Renewable EnergyAccess.com is a Web publication covering the alternative energy industry. Michael Eckhart is president of the American Council on Renewable Energy.

2. Calvin R. Trice, "Residents in Highland Vent about Wind Farm," *Richmond Times-Dispatch,* May 21, 2005.

3. "An Assessment of the Available Windy Land Area and Wind Energy Potential in the Contiguous United States," Pacific Northwest Laboratory, 1991. Available from American Wind Energy Association, www.awea.org.

4. Fay and Golumb, *Energy and the Environment,* 166–67.

5. Mick Sagrillo, interview with the author. Measurements include examples of wind systems found advertised for sale in 2008.

6. Steve Raabe, "Elbert Couple Cuts Energy Bills with Small Wind Turbine," *Denver Post,* May 18, 2005.

Chapter 4—Other Technologies: Fuel Cells, Biodiesel Fuel, and Geothermal Heat Pumps

1. Katie Mulik, *The News Hour with Jim Lehrer,* October 20, 2003, www.pbs.org/newshour/science/hydrogen/environment .html.

2. *The Hydrogen Economy: Opportunities, Costs, Barriers, and*

R&D Needs (Washington, DC: National Academies Press, 2004), 45. (www.nap.edu/books)

3. *Energy Independence Now*, Santa Monica, California, fact sheet on hydrogen fuel cells, "What Is A Fuel Cell and How Does It Work?" See also www.fuelcells.org.

4. Fay and Golumb, *Energy and the Environment,* 65.

5. See the State of California's Web page on the Hydrogen Highway, www.hydrogenhighway.ca.gov.

6. Ulrike Schramm, public relations manager, SFC Smart Fuel Cell AG, telephone interview with the author: May 19, 2007. Peter Podesser, CEO, SFC Smart Fuel Cell AG, telephone interview with the author, June 4, 2008. For information on buying this type of fuel cell, see www.sandpipertech.com.

7. Hydrogenics Corporation of Mississauga, Ontario, "Hydrogenics Signs Contract to Provide Fuel Cell System for U.S. Army Armoured Vehicle," May 25, 2005. Hydrogenics is a fuel-cell developer.

8. Kettering University, Flint, Michigan, "Greening Public Transportation," October 12, 2007. See www.kettering.edu.

9. Seth Dunn, "Hydrogen Futures: Toward a Sustainable Energy System," *Worldwatch Institute Paper 157* (Washington, DC: Worldwatch Institute, August 2001).

10. Natural Resources Defense Council, www.nrdc.org.

11. World Fuel Cell Council, based in Germany, www.fuelcell world.org.

12. Dunn, "Hydrogen Futures," 7–8.

13. Kunstler, "The Long Emergency," as excerpted in *Rolling Stone,* March 2005.

14. World Fuel Cell Council, www.fuelcellworld.org.

15. National Public Radio, *Science Friday,* June 6, 2008.

16. Jim Motavalli, "Putting the Hindenburg to Rest," *The New York Times,* June 5, 2005, sec. 12, p. 1.

17. Alternative Fuels Data Center of the U.S. Department of Energy's Energy Efficiency and Renewable Energy program, www.eere.energy.gov.

18. "Heat Your Home with Biodiesel," *Mother Earth News,* no. 201, December–January, 2004.

19. Nevin Christensen, interview with the author, May 2005.

20. Throughout this section, I have relied heavily on information from the California Energy Commission in Sacramento, which offers a wealth of information and facts through its Web site, known as the Consumer Energy Center, www.consumer energycenter.org.

21. George Goodrich, telephone interview with the author, July 3, 2008.

22. Joel N. Gordes, telephone interview with the author, July 3, 2008.

23. Gordes, July 3, 2008.

Chapter 5—Heating with Wood

1. United States Environmental Protection Agency, Technology Transfer Network Air Toxics Web site, www.epa.gov/ttn/atw/hlthef/polycycl.html.

2. Lawrence H. Fisher, James E. Houck, Paul E. Tiegs, and James McGaughey, *Long-Term Performance of EPA-Certified Phase 2 Woodstoves: Klamath Falls and Portland, Oregon* (Cincinnati, Ohio: National Risk Management Research Laboratory, 1998–1999).

3. U.S. Department of Energy, Office of Energy Efficiency and Renewable Energy, online consumer fact sheet on heating with wood, www.eere.energy.gov.

4. Maine's Department of Environmental Protection, explaining

EPA regulations, www.maine.gov/dep/air/education/woodstv.htm.

5. Summarizing the argument neatly is consumer advocate Debra Lynn Dadd in "Why Wood Is the Best Fuel," www.worldwise.com.

6. University of New Hampshire Climate Education Initiative, UNH Greenhouse Gas Emissions Inventory 1990–2003 (Durham: University of New Hampshire, July 2004). UNH cites the U.S. Environmental Protection Agency.

7. Dirk Thomas of Cuttingsville, Vermont, telephone interview with the author. Thomas is the author of *The Wood Burner's Companion* (Chambersburg, PA: Allen C. Hood, 2004). John Bartok, of Ashford, Connecticut, a retired agricultural engineer with the University of Connecticut, telephone interview with the author, April 2005.

8. "The End of the Wood Stove? An Interview with Dan Melcon, Industry Gadfly and Fellow Alarmist," *Mother Earth News*, Issue 170, October–November 1998.

9. Stephen Broderick, University of Connecticut Cooperative Extension forester, e-mail interview with the author, June 2005.

10. "Home Heating with Wood," Clemson University Cooperative Extension Service, May 1988.

11. John and Martha Storey, *Storey's Basic Country Skills* (Pownal, VT: Storey Publishing, 1999), 61.

12. Don Hopey, "Wood Treatment Linked to Dangers," *Pittsburgh Post-Gazette,* January 25, 1998.

13. For a fair assessment of pellet stoves, I suggest searching the "Ask Umbra" column in the online magazine *Grist,* www.grist.org/topic/Ask_Umbra. For a consumer-oriented discussion of pellet stoves, see www.alternative-heating-info.com.

14. Bartok, April 2005.

Chapter 6—Harnessing a Backyard Stream: Micro-Hydroelectric Systems

1. U.S. Department of Energy, Office of Energy Efficiency and Renewable Energy, information about the hydroelectric program of the U.S. Department of Energy, Wind and Water Technologies Program, www.eere.energy.gov/windandhydro/.

2. For background about dams and hydroelectric plants, I consulted E.C. Pielou, *Fresh Water* (Chicago: University of Chicago Press, 1998). Information about the Hoover Dam is from the U.S. Bureau of Reclamation, www.usbr.gov/lc/hooverdam/faqs/powerfaq.html. Information about the Grand Coulee Dam is from http://users.owt.com/chubbard/gcdam.

3. Paul Cunningham and Barbara Atkinson, "Micro Hydro Power in the 1990s," *Home Power,* no. 44, December 1994–January 1995, 24–29. Juliette and Lucien Gunderman, "Powerful Dreams: Crown Hill Farm's Hydro Electric Plant," *Home Power,* no. 96, August–September 2003, 14–21. Dan New, "Intro to Hydro Power," *Home Power,* no. 103, October–November 2004, 14–20.

Chapter 7—Alternative Cars

1. "Potential Impacts of Climate Change on U.S. Transportation: Special Report 290," Committee on Climate Change and U.S. Transportation, National Research Council, 2008.

2. Edison Electric Institute, www.eei.org, offers a good overview of the Energy Independence and Security Act of 2007. Background on gas mileage of the national fleet came from author's interview with Jeff Deyette, Union of Concerned Scientists in Boston, June 2005. Model T Ford gas mileage from www.wanttoknow.info.

3. Renewable Energy Lab, Golden, Colorado, www.nrel.gov.

4. Amory B. Lovins, "Getting Off Oil: Recent Leaps and Next Steps," Rocky Mountain Institute spring 2008 newsletter, vol. xxiv, No. 1.

5. Connecticut General Assembly, Special Act No. 05-06, "An Act Concerning a Connecticut Clean Car Incentive Program," June 24, 2005.

6. Jim Motavalli, "What a Gas! A Week in Suburbia with a Hydrogen Honda," *The New York Times*, June 5, 2005, sec. 12, p. 1.

7. "How a Hybrid Works," Edmunds.com, the Web car magazine. See www.edmunds.com.

8. "How a Hybrid Works."

9. "How a Hybrid Works."

10. Bill Kwong, interview with the author, July 3, 2008.

11. Kwong, July 3, 2008.

12. "As Gas Prices Pinch, Support for Energy Exploration Rises," Pew Research Center for People and the Press survey, July 1, 2008. "Amid record gas prices, public support for greater energy exploration is spiking. Compared with just a few months ago, many more Americans are giving higher priority to more energy exploration, rather than more conservation. An increasing proportion also says that developing new sources of energy—rather than protecting the environment—is the more important national priority." See http://people-press.org.

13. Gas mileage and efficiency rankings for regular and hybrid cars are from www.edmunds.com.

Chapter 8—Conservation: Not a New Idea

1. "ExxonMobil 2007 Summary Annual Report," Irving, Texas, 16.

2. For a somewhat goofy description of how electricity is made and what is lost as it travels to a house, see Patricia Nelson Limerick, Claudia Puska, Andrew Hildner, et al., "So You Want to Make Toast?" in *What Every Westerner Should Know About Energy* (Boulder, CO: Center of the American West, 2003), 1–2.

3. Kimberley A. Strassel, "State of Change: Arnold Schwarzenegger on California's place in the new gold rush," *Wall Street Journal*, March 24, 2008, R3.

4. For more on cap-and-trade programs, see Pew Center for Climate Change, *Climate Change 101: Understanding and Responding to Global Climate Change* (Arlington, Virginia, undated), www.pewclimate.org.

5. "The Elusive Negawatt," *The Economist*, May 8, 2008

6. "The Elusive Negawatt," *The Economist*, May 8, 2008. "Among American states, for every cent per kilowatt-hour by which prices exceed the national average, energy consumption drops by about 7 percent of the average."

7. David Leonhardt, Jad Mouawad, and David E. Sanger, "To Conserve Gas, President Calls for Less Driving," *The New York Times*, September 27, 2005, A1.

8. James Brooke, "Is a Salaryman without a Suit Like Sushi without the Rice?" *The New York Times*, May 20, 2005, A1, C4.

9. Allen Best, "How Dense Can We Be," *High Country News*, June 13, 2005, p. 10–11.

10. Best, "How Dense Can We Be," 11.

11. Christine Woodside, "Oasis on the Edge," *Hartford Courant*, September 7, 2003, C4.

12. U.S. Department of Energy, Office of Energy Efficiency and Renewable Energy, Energy Savers, www.eere.energy.gov/consumer/tips/.

13. Kenneth T. Jackson, "Public Transportation: The Twentieth Century," *The Reader's Companion to American History*, http://

college.hmco.com/history/readerscomp/rcah/html/ah_072007_thetwentieth.htm.

14. See the Web sites www.pbs.org/americaswalking and www.walktoschool.org.

15. Lindsey Grant, *The Collapsing Bubble: Growth and Fossil Energy* (Santa Ana, CA: Seven Locks Press, 2005), 5.

16. "Low Cost, Abundant Energy: Paradise Lost?" *Science,* v. 184, no. 4134 (April 19, 1974). I cite the version anthologized in *Readings on Energy Conservation: Selected Materials Compiled by the Congressional Research Service at the Request of Henry M. Jackson, Chairman, Committee on Interior and Insular Affairs, United States Senate* (Washington, DC: U.S. Government Printing Office, 1975).

17. Gary Althen, *American Ways: A Guide for Foreigners in the United States* (Yarmouth, Maine: Intercultural Press, 2002).

18. Paul Cunningham, telephone interview with the author, June 2005.

19. Cunningham, June 2005.

20. Cunningham, June 2005.

21. Elliot Aronson and Michael O'Leary, "The Relative Effectiveness of Models and Prompts on Energy Conservation: A Field Experiment in a Shower Room." *Journal of Environmental Systems,* 12, 219–224. This study is cited in numerous research papers.

22. Chauncey Starr, "Realities of the Energy Crisis," in *Perspectives on Energy: Issues, Ideas, and Environmental Dilemmas,* ed. Lon C. Ruedisili and Morris W. Firebaugh (New York: Oxford University Press, 1975).

Chapter 10—An Appliance Manifesto

1. For Walt Disney's impact on how we view modern appliances, valuing convenience in appliances, go to www.yesterland.com/progress.html.

2. Jeff Holyfield, director of news and information, Consumers Energy, Jackson, Michigan, interview with the author.

3. "Inventory of U.S. Greenhouse Gas Emissions and Sinks: 1990—2005" (April 2007), U.S. Environmental Protection Agency #430-R-07-002, www.epa.gov/climatechange/emissions/usinventoryreport.html.

4. U.S. Department of Energy, Energy Information Administration, *Annual Energy Outlook 2008,* see www.eia.doe.gov/oiaf/aeo/index.html.

5. To calculate the electricity appliances use, I followed the instructions of the U.S. Department of Energy, Office of Energy Efficiency and Renewable Energy. See www.eere.energy.gov/consumer/your_home/appliances/index.cfm/mytopic=10040. Check the list of common appliances for the range of watts each one puts out. Or, to be more accurate, check the labels or manuals that came with your appliances. Multiply wattage by the number of hours the appliance runs each day. Divide this number by 1,000 to calculate the daily kilowatt-hour use, as 1,000 watts equals 1 kilowatt. Finally, multiply this by the number of days you use the appliance each year. You then can calculate your yearly cost to own this appliance by multiplying the kilowatt-hours-per-year figure by your local electricity rate per kilowatt-hour.

Index

About the Author

Christine Woodside is an environmental writer and editor. Her articles on energy, conservation, and American life have appeared in many periodicals, including the *New York Times*, the *Hartford Courant*, the *Washington Post*, *Audubon*, *Woman's Day*, the *Yale Climate Media Forum*, and others. She has spoken about citizen energy conservation to the employees of the National Renewable Energy Lab. She edits the journal *Appalachia* and lives in Deep River, Connecticut.